The Wreck of the ABERGAVENNY

Peele Castle in a Storm, by Sir George Beaumont

ALSO BY ALETHEA HAYTER

Mrs Browning: A Poet's Work and its Setting

A Sultry Month: Scenes of London Literary Life in 1846

Elizabeth Barrett Browning

Opium and the Romantic Imagination

Horatio's Version

A Voyage in Vain: Coleridge's Journey to Malta in 1804

*A Wise Woman: A Memoir of Lavinia Mynors from
her Letters and Diaries*

Charlotte Yonge

AS EDITOR

*Fitzgerald to his Friends: Selected Letters of
Edward Fitzgerald*

*Portrait of Friendship: New Letters of James Russell
Lowell to Sybella Lady Lyttelton, 1881–1891*

*The Backbone: Diaries of a Military Family in the
Napoleonic Wars*

ALETHEA HAYTER

The Wreck of the
ABERGAVENNY

MACMILLAN

First published 2002 by Macmillan
an imprint of Pan Macmillan Ltd
Pan Macmillan, 20 New Wharf Road, London N1 9RR
Basingstoke and Oxford
Associated companies throughout the world
www.panmacmillan.com

ISBN 0 333 98917 1

9 8 7 6 5 4 3 2 1

A CIP catalogue record for this book is available from
the British Library.

Typeset by Intype London Ltd
Printed and bound in Great Britain by
Mackays of Chatham plc, Chatham, Kent

'How do you turn catastrophe into art?'

Julian Barnes
*A History of the World
in 10½ Chapters*

'Not without hope we suffer and we mourn.'

William Wordsworth
*Elegiac Stanzas Suggested by
a Picture of Peele Castle*

Contents

List of Illustrations

Foreword and Acknowledgements

The line between biography and fiction has now become blurred, but readers still have the right to know whether they are being presented with fact or invention, especially in a biographical sketch like this one, without reference notes which would have enabled a sceptical reader to check with the original sources of the evidence for each event. Readers may be assured that everything in this book presented as fact is taken from letters, diaries, official records, newspapers and pamphlets contemporary with the people and incidents described, with no fictional additions or inventions – or at any rate none by me; some of the newspapers and pamphlets quoted may contain rumours and exaggerations about the main events in the story, but unless these are demonstrably untrue, I have included them at face value, as what was believed or surmised at the time. Speculations and logical deductions about motives and emotions, from the point of view of today's hindsight, have been distinguished from evidence about them from contemporary records. The sub-text of this biography is a pattern of how events are transmuted as they are recorded by eyewitnesses, by family and friends, by poets and historians, biographers and journalists, in search of truth, mitigation or excitement.

The known details of John Wordsworth's life are given in full in Carl H. Ketcham's thoroughly researched introduction and notes in his 1969 edition of John Wordsworth's letters, which has been the main source for this study, together with Ernest de Selincourt's and Chester L. Shaver's superbly annotated 1967 edition of the letters of William and Dorothy Wordsworth. Much information about the East India Company and its ships has been taken from Hosea B. Morse's *Chronicles of The East India Company Trading to China* and C. Northcote Parkinson's *Trade in the Eastern Seas*.

I should like to thank Ed Cumming – whose group, the Chelmsford Underwater Archaeological Unit, has conducted on-going exploration of the site of the wreck of the *Abergavenny* – for much helpful information and advice. Mr Cumming is the author of a detailed, but as yet unpublished, account of the wreck and the salvage from it, which has included many fascinating artefacts recovered by the Chelmsford team (see Plates 11–15).

I should also like to thank Dr Robert Woof, Director of the Wordsworth Trust, and the staff of the Dove Cottage library for guidance and help in finding unpublished records of John Wordsworth and the wreck of the *Abergavenny*. For help in tracking down contemporary pamphlets, logbooks and illustrations I am grateful to Linda Shirley, Senior Librarian, and the staff of Weymouth Library; to the staffs of the East India Office Collection in the British Library, the National Maritime Museum, the Public Record Office, the Tate Gallery, and Julia Nurse of the Prints and Drawings Department, British Museum. Among friends who have aided me on visits to carry out research for this book are Jasmine Blakeway and Sophia Gray; Claire Tomalin guided me through the horrors of modern technology to master the British Library's new computers; I am very grateful to all of them.

Permission to quote from copyright texts has been given by the Clarendon Press for William and Dorothy Wordsworth, *Letters: The Early Years*, vol. I, ed. E. de Selincourt and C. L. Shaver, 1967; Samuel Taylor Coleridge, *Collected Letters*, vol. III, ed. E. L. Griggs, 1959; Mary Moorman, *William Wordsworth*, vol. II, 1965; by Routledge & Kegan Paul for Samuel Taylor Coleridge, *Notebooks*, vol. II, ed. Kathleen Coburn, 1962; by Cornell University Press for John Wordsworth, *Letters*, ed. Carl H. Ketcham, 1969; Charles and Mary Lamb, *Letters*, vol. II, ed. E. W. Marre, 1976; by the Trustees of the Wordsworth Trust for unpublished letters and map.

Permission to reproduce paintings, drawings, engravings, maps and photographs has been given by the Leicester City Museum, the British Library, the Wordsworth Trust, the Tate Gallery, the Weymouth Library, the Fogg Art Museum, Ed Cumming/ Chelmsford Underwater Archaeology Unit, Imray Laurie Norie and Wilson Ltd, and Brian Taylor of Wyke Regis.

Prologue ~ Picture of a shipwreck

WILLIAM WORDSWORTH stands looking at a seascape painted by his friend Sir George Beaumont, a picture of a place that he knew, a rocky coast with a ship in a bay. He imagines how it would have been painted if it represented the scene as he remembers it. The sea would have been glassy calm, the sky clear, the air windless, the sunshine radiant – a vision of an invulnerable peace and bliss that would last for ever. But the actual picture that he is looking at is very different. The location is the same, but lowering over the rugged coast there is a pitch-black veil of storm clouds, opening at the horizon on a glaring patch of sky, across which a flash of lightning zigzags. Wild waves are breaking, and caught among them out to sea is a foundering ship. Here there is no promise of peace or lasting happiness; those were unreal dreams, Wordsworth now recognizes. Real life is full of storm and fear like this picture; can something good, some gain of fortitude and control, come out of experiencing such suffering as this?

PART ONE

LAUNCHING

Chapter One

'I HAVE THE PLEASURE to inform you that the Abergany is arrived safe at Portsmouth and if the Wind continues fair which it is at present I shall expect to leave this place tomorrow' wrote Captain John Wordsworth to his brother William on 24 January 1805. He was thirty-three years old and was captain of the *Earl of Abergavenny* (which he pronounced and spelt as Abergany), a handsome 1200-ton merchant ship of the East India Company, bound for India and China with 400 hundred men and women – crew, passengers and troops – on board and a rich cargo of silver dollars and luxurious goods *[Plate 1]*. The wind indeed seemed fair for John Wordsworth, with every prospect of a voyage which would make him wealthy enough to retire and join his brother and sister in Westmorland.

John Wordsworth had been captain of the *Earl of Abergavenny* since 1801, and in the East India Company's maritime service for seventeen years, ever since as a sixteen-year-old boy he had left his family in Westmorland to embark on a life at sea. Born in December 1772, he was the fourth child of an attorney; two brothers, Richard and William, and a sister, Dorothy, preceded him; one more son, Christopher, was to follow. By the time he was twelve, both his parents were dead, and he and his siblings were living with their mother's parents under a restrictive and unsympathetic regime which knitted the five children more closely together. Dorothy was devoted to John, 'the kindest and most affectionate of brothers', but she was apt to refer to him as 'poor dear John' or 'poor fellow' in her letters. He was, she said, considered something of a dunce compared with his cleverer brothers. 'He has a most excellent heart, he is not so bright as either William or Christopher but he has very good commonsense and is very well calculated for the profession he has chosen.'

That profession was a life at sea; there seems to have been no consideration that he might go on to a university like his brothers, and after spending six years at Hawkshead Grammar School where all the brothers were educated, he was given a brief training in navigation and was then launched into a career in the East India Company's maritime service by the influence of his father's cousins Captain John Wordsworth senior and Thomas Robinson. Dorothy's comment on his departure was, 'My brother John has set sail for Barbadoes. I hope, poor Lad! that he will be successful and happy, he is much delighted with the profession he has chosen.'

She knew that her brother John was not really a dunce. He was called one because 'he loved his own solitary dreamings, wanderings with his fishing rod, or social Boyish sports, better than his master's tasks'. Solitary dreaming was the essence of John's nature, he found it difficult to communicate with other people, even sometimes with his nearest family and friends after a separation, till he had been with them again for some time. Most of the time he withdrew into a meditative reserve, which was seen as shyness even by his own family. His brother William described him as 'shy even to disease' and his father nick-named him, as a child, 'the Ibex', because that species of mountain goat was reputedly the shyest of all animals. His habits from his childhood were, said Dorothy, 'shy and lonely in the extreme, so that if he had not had so much dignity of character he would to most have appeared odd'. That he did so appear is witnessed by a rumour told by Coleridge's daughter (perhaps emanating from her mother, who was not disposed to praise any of the Wordsworths) that John 'was thought heavy and commonplace by general observers'. She speculated that 'his shyness and taciturnity evidenced a something peculiar in his nervous system'. It has been suggested that harsh treatment by his grandparents when he was a child, and his brothers' superior talents, made him feel an unwanted dunce, who would never make any mark in life, and caused him to set up a defensive wall of reserve behind which he could hide and dream. But the few surviving letters in which we can hear his voice reveal enough of fun, often self-mocking, of admiring affection for others, especially for his poet brother, of strong moral convictions, to exculpate him from being neurotically obsessed by feelings of inadequacy.

This silent sixteen-year-old embarked on a life of worldwide travel, adventures and encounters which gave him a far wider experience than his clever brothers were ever to achieve. In the next twelve years he sailed to Barbados, Jamaica, the USA, the Azores, India and three times to China, in various ships including a previous *Earl of Abergavenny* under his cousin, Captain John Wordsworth senior. He was regularly promoted: fifth mate in 1793, fourth mate in 1795, second mate in 1797. Before an officer in the Company's service could get a command of an East Indiaman, he had to be over twenty-five and to have completed a voyage of over twenty months to India or China. The normal promotion ladder involved a first voyage as fifth or sixth mate, a second as third or fourth mate and a third as first or second mate, so John's career rises were satisfactory but not spectacular.

Most of these voyages took place while England was at war with France. John's attitude to this was robust; his last promotion prompted the reflection, 'It is an ill wind they say that blows nobody any good luck. The longer this war continues the better it will be for me.' This now sounds unpleasantly bellicose, until we remember the good-hearted Admiral Croft in Jane Austen's *Persuasion* blithely hoping that 'we have the good luck to live to another war'. War was not then the universal dread that it is now; it was regarded as the preserve of professionals, who enjoyed exercising their skills and making their fortunes, and had comparatively little impact on civilians, in England at any rate. John told Charles Lamb that his heart's desire was to meet a Frenchman on the seas, and Lamb long remembered his exultation at the thought. Like all merchant captains during the Napoleonic Wars, he was restricted by having to sail in convoy with a warship escort, by having members of his crew press-ganged for the Navy, in home ports or in the Far East, and, as he was to find some years later, by being in danger of capture by a French squadron. In his letters he seldom referred to the wider interests of the war; his mind was concentrated on running his own ship.

For a man with his temperament, he was an unexpectedly firm disciplinarian. The logbooks of the *Earl of Abergavenny* on her China voyages under his command regularly record him as having ordered seamen to be given a dozen or two dozen lashes, or put in irons. But these were not for trivial offences. The men in question were guilty not only of insolence, disobedience and drunkenness, but more heinously of theft, striking an officer, trying to stab a fellow-seaman, hiding in a shore boat in a bid to desert, even mutiny. On one occasion, faced with an insolent and near-mutinous crew of recently-recruited men at the start of a voyage, he did not hesitate to award floggings to the ringleaders. But these punishments were decreed after consultations with his officers, and were in accordance with regulations which were read out during the voyage to the ship's company, who therefore knew what to expect if they offended. John Wordsworth was a firm but just captain, not a sadist.

He could be crotchety and ironical in his dislike of some people and things. Clumsiness or muddle roused his temper from its usual mildness, and so did improper contradiction by his subordinates. Surveying his officers on his first voyage in command of the *Earl of Abergavenny*, he pronounced them 'very good *young men*, the eldest about three and twenty, but I do not like them the worse for that. They will be more *obedient* and less *knowing*.' He was sometimes irascible about lapses in taste and consideration for others; when he heard that a beautiful grove of trees in Grasmere had been cut down, his resentment at this offence was such that he declared that if he had the 'monster' who had committed it in his power 'in *my* ship ... I would give him a tight flogging'. Ecological campaigners who today drive spikes into tree-trunks to snag the chainsaws and mutilate the arms of men who are trying to cut down the trees may find themselves in sympathy with John Wordsworth's idea of a suitable punishment.

This martinet stance makes John sound like a conventional rough and hearty mariner, but he was far from being that. He was always uneasy at first contact with strangers, it made him feel hurried and queer, he owned. Dealing with tradesmen and shipping offices was to be the most difficult and uncongenial part of his job when he became a captain; 'being a new thing I find myself a little at a loss – I do not go on so well as an old experienced Capt. would do.' He found social visits unpleasant, was little used to general company, and loathed intrusive gossip. Even with his own officers he was not at ease; he would not go with them or even with his fellow commanders for convivial evenings on shore, when his ship was in port, but stayed on board and read poetry instead. His brother William said of him that 'being accustomed to live with Men with whom he had little sympathy, and who did not value or understand what he valued . . . [he] had lived all his life with the deepest part of his nature shut up within himself'. This aloofness puzzled his shipmates, who nicknamed him 'The Philosopher'.

His life on board during the long voyages to the Far East (the passage from England to India might take six months, and the round trip to China and back nearly two years) was a solitude encapsulated in a crowded community. Any ship's captain, whatever his personality, had to keep a certain distance between himself and everyone else on board, but with John the distance was greater and colder. He had to be with the ship's company for a captain's normal duties. The *Abergavenny*'s logbooks convey the monotonous regime of his long weeks and months at sea as he ordered the guns to be exercised, had the sails adjusted as calms succeeded squalls, dictated signals to passing homeward-bound ships, read out the Articles of War to the crew, conducted Divine Service on Sunday mornings or funeral rites for the burial at sea of men who had died of sickness or of falls from the topsail yards. When his superintendence of the ship's management was not required, he would pace the windward side of the quarterdeck, which on all East Indiamen was reserved for the captain, and might not be entered uninvited by anyone else. Years later William recreated in a poem a vision of his brother treading to and fro

> . . . unwearied and alone
> In that habitual restlessness of foot
> His short domain upon the vessel's deck
> While she pursues her course through the dreary sea.

John was a stargazer, a watchful observer of waves and clouds and moonlight at sea, of mountains and trees and flowers on land, which he saw with 'an eye practised like a blind man's touch', in full sympathy with his brother's and sister's passion for Nature, indeed himself a '*silent* Poet' as William called him.

When he was not dreamily pacing the deck, he was reading in his cabin. Poetry was what he read most. When he was a child, his father had made him and his siblings learn by heart passages from Spenser, Shakespeare and Milton, and when he became a sailor he took to sea with him a library of English poetry, partly chosen on William's advice. He brooded on Shakespeare's plays and whether their subtleties of imagination and characterization could ever be conveyed to the audience by actors in London theatres. But although he could write that 'Shakespeare is the only man I like at present' he was forced to add 'yet one cannot for a voyage of sixteen months constantly *stick* to him', and he decided to experiment with Spenser for a change.

The work of another poet, a modern one near and dear to John, his brother William, preoccupied him on many long days at sea. He had with him copies of all the poems William had completed so far; Dorothy sent him packets bulging with further copies, and he had copies of each edition of the published *Lyrical Ballads*. William wrote into a notebook a special collection of his poems for John to take to sea,

> To travel with him night and day,
> And in his private hearing say
> Refreshing things, whatever way
> His weary Vessel went.

William was convinced that his writings, printed and manuscript, were 'the delight and one of the chief solaces' of his brother's long voyages, and John did get much refreshment and pleasure out of his brother's poetry. There are many references in his letters to the poems he liked best, to their reception by critics and the public, to the publication of the second edition of the *Lyrical Ballads* which he helped to negotiate on William's behalf with the publisher Longmans, while he was in London between voyages. Even a rather hostile witness, Coleridge's daughter Sara, who believed John Wordsworth was commonplace and neurotically taciturn, gave him credit as a discerning critic of Wordsworth's poems, not merely with a 'brother's partiality' but with real insight.

For the first twelve years of his life at sea, this thoughtful self-contained man kept in touch with his siblings chiefly by letter, though the war made postal deliveries from distant ports unreliable. Only two of his letters during this period survive, one to his eldest brother Richard and one to his uncle Christopher Crackanthorpe. Dorothy's letters during these years mention some letters received from him, and news of his movements, but both he and she expressed anxiety about absence of news of each other when he was at sea. Between voyages he had brief meetings with Richard, William and Dorothy in 1789, spent four months with Dorothy at their uncle William Cookson's house in Norfolk in 1791–2, and then went north to stay with relations and have a seaside and walking holiday with his younger brother Christopher; and late in 1799 he joined William and Coleridge on a walking tour of the Lake District. But these widely-spaced contacts had not yet made William, Dorothy and John really intimate; he saw more of his unsympathetic eldest brother Richard, the attorney, who was based in London where John could easily drop in on him between voyages, than he did of William and Dorothy, who in these years had no permanent home of their own in which to receive him, and were constantly on the move. When, as in 1797, they could have made a temporary home for him at Racedown, the spacious house in Dorset which they were then occupying – 'Poor John! How glad I should have been to see him here' wrote Dorothy to Richard – he was on board the East Indiaman *Duke of Montrose* as second mate, anchored in the Downs with a mutinous crew at the start of a voyage to Calcutta. In these years it was Dorothy who felt the strongest ties with John and her other brothers; the afflictions of their childhood, the loss of their parents and their patrimony, had, she wrote, 'all contributed to bind us closer by the bonds of affection, notwithstanding we have

Chapter Two

JUST BEFORE CHRISTMAS 1799 William and
Dorothy took possession of Dove Cottage, Grasmere,
[Plate 2] and for the first time had a settled home of
their own, and could invite John to spend his leave
with them between voyages *[Plates 3 and 4]*. Dorothy
had not seen him for seven years, and though
William had been with him recently at a family
funeral and on a brief walking tour, he had not yet
begun to feel that he and his brother, seen only by
'glimpses' for twelve years, could fully understand
and harmonize with each other.

> Year followed year, my Brother! and we two,
> Conversing not, knew little in what mould
> Each other's mind was fashioned; and at length
> When once again we met in Grasmere Vale,
> Between us there was little other bond
> Than common feelings of fraternal love.

If William felt like this before John arrived at Grasmere in January 1800 to be reunited with his family,

the diffident John felt it still more strongly as he drew near to Dove Cottage. 'Twice did he approach the door and lay his hand upon the latch, and stop, and turn away without the courage to enter ... he then went to the Inn and sent us word that he was come,' Dorothy told a friend after John's death, adding, 'this will give you a notion of the depths of his affections, and the delicacy of his feelings'.

Their misgivings were unnecessary. It became apparent almost at once – when John had been summoned from the inn – that he, Dorothy, William and Mary Hutchinson, friend of them all since childhood and then staying at Dove Cottage, were all going to fit in perfectly with each others' ways and share their enthusiasms. Mere 'common feelings of fraternal love' quickly turned into a far stronger bond between like-moulded minds, so that John began to see that here was his home and his future, once he had made enough money from his voyages to give William and Dorothy a secure future, and himself somewhere near at hand to which he could eventually retire, and spend the rest of his life in their company. He had always put William's advancement before his own, and had felt that any money in the Wordsworth family should be concentrated on financing William's education and poetic vocation. As far back as 1787, before he started his career at sea, he had declared that he himself would need very little out of his father's estate, and that all the rest should go to pay for William's studies and training. Twelve years later, just before the move to Dove Cottage, he had offered William £40 to buy land on which to build a cottage at Grasmere. Now that he was seeing and sharing William's way of life at Dove Cottage, his ideas for their future were crystallizing. 'He encouraged me', said William, 'to persist in the plan of life which I had adopted; "I will work for you", was his language, "and you shall attempt to do something for the world. Could I but see you with a green field of your own and a Cow and two or three other little comforts I shall be happy." ' On their side, William and Dorothy delighted in the expectation that John would eventually come 'to live among us the life he loved'.

That life was an outdoor one of long, long walks, sometimes alone, sometimes with one or more of the others; of swimming in the lakes, of gardening, of planting trees, of fishing. A favourite walk of his when alone was Lady Wood, a grove of firs on the east shore of the Grasmere lake, just above Town End, where by constant pacing he wore a path through the undergrowth. William only discovered this hidden retreat later, and the wood then became 'John's Grove' to the family, and William in his turn used to pace along the path worn by John, imagining that he might be timing his steps to John's on the deck of his far-distant ship, and composing verses about the longed-for day

When we, and others whom we love, shall meet
A second time, in Grasmere's happy Vale.

On his walks John's fine eye observed, and pointed out to his companions, the smallest details that brightened the landscape. Even at midnight he would call Dorothy out into the garden to see the moonlight in the valley, or a sky of clouds or brilliant stars.

Within the cottage John's sympathy and helpfulness were also evident in those months. It was still sparsely furnished and uncomfortable, with bare walls, stone-flagged floors and smoking chimneys. John's bedroom was a small box with one high-up window, no curtains to the bed, and walls covered with newspapers pasted on by Dorothy. But John loved the cottage, he paced its stone floors rejoicing that 'his Father's Children had once again a home together'. He was interested in all Dorothy's housekeeping cares and needs, and unobtrusively did many dexterous carpentry jobs on shelves and door-locks to make them all more comfortable.

'A mind of usefulness and ingenuity seemed to furnish him with constant employment within. He drew, he varnished, he carpentered, he glued'; 'he was evidently a young man of considerable taste in reading, though principally in poetry' – those two descriptions might be a composite of John Wordsworth's personality, but they are of course Jane Austen's pictures of two other naval officers, Captains

Harville and Benwick in *Persuasion*. In a book published in 1971, a preposterous suggestion was made
that John Wordsworth was the nameless lover whom
Jane Austen met by the seaside, and might have
married had he not died a few months later. The
only evidence for the existence of this lover was a
reminiscence told by Cassandra Austen, many years
later, to her niece Caroline, and a third-hand story
said to be from Austen family tradition, that in
Switzerland Jane Austen met and loved a naval
officer who shortly afterwards died of brain fever.
The lover of whom Cassandra spoke may have been a
clergyman whom her sister met in Devonshire in 1801;
it certainly was not John Wordsworth, who was on
the other side of the world, sailing to and from China,
during all the seaside holidays which Jane Austen
spent in Dorset and Devonshire in 1801–5. Neither
he nor she ever went to Switzerland, which in any
case is not the most plausible venue for a seaside
romance. But this foolish suggestion does bring to
mind that Jane Austen had two brothers in the Royal
Navy, and had met several of their shipmates. She
used her observation of such ways of naval officers
as their handiness and their poetic tastes, to create
two fictional characters; they and their real-life contemporary John Wordsworth reinforce each other in
the reader's imagination.

John Wordsworth as Jane Austen's lover is a myth,
but there was a woman whom he loved. A month

after John arrived at Dove Cottage in January 1800 Mary Hutchinson came to stay there again, and remained for five weeks. She was a tall healthy-looking woman with an aquiline nose; her eyes were deep-set under elegant eyebrows, but one of them had a squint. This did not seem displeasing, said De Quincey, in a woman whose winning benignity of manner captivated everybody. They all loved and admired Mary; she was a woman of few words but ready smiles, of warm and gracious kindness, affectionate, unselfish and loyal.

William 'had no thought of marriage' in 1800, he later declared; his entanglement with Annette Vallon still had to be sorted out. Mary Hutchinson and John, rather than Mary and William, seemed to be paired in everyone's eyes during those early spring weeks when they were together in Dove Cottage. John 'affectionately loved' Mary, Dorothy remembered, he 'used to walk with her everywhere, and they were exceedingly attached to each other'. William thought that John found in the company of Mary, as well as of his siblings, 'all that was wanting to make him completely happy'. Mary herself was later to say, 'John was the first who led me to everything that I love in this neighbourhood.'

Whether Mary Hutchinson was at all in love with John that spring will never be known. It has been maintained that she had always, since her childhood, loved William, that they had a secret understanding that they would marry eventually, but that lack of money and the Annette Vallon affair prevented them at this time from being openly engaged. John seems then to have had no idea of any such connection, and if he did not declare his own feelings to Mary then, he was not consciously stepping down in order not to stand in William's way. He may have felt that he too was financially in no position to marry yet, but there is sufficient evidence on his side that he loved Mary, whatever her feelings may have been. She perhaps saw him simply as an extremely congenial sympathetic friend; he certainly saw her as more than that. He wrote to her seventeen times between October 1800 and September 1802, addressing her as 'dearest Mary' and signing himself 'thine affectionate Friend'. He re-read her letters to him a dozen times a day, everything that she could tell him about herself and her doings would be welcome, he wrote to her twice in one evening because he could not 'forgo the pleasure of talking to you a little again'. Then in September 1802, on return from his first voyage to China as captain, he met William and Dorothy in London and heard (perhaps from a letter from Mary which had been awaiting his return) that in the previous autumn she and William had become engaged to be married. Then, at the end of a letter from Dorothy to Mary, he wrote, 'I have been reading your letter over and over again My Dearest Mary till tears have come into my eyes and I know not how to

William's engagement to Mary. His trading on his own account for this voyage had been partly financed by a loan from Dorothy from a recent legacy, in return for which he undertook to pay her £20 a year, an important contribution to the meagre finances of the Dove Cottage menage, and one whose irregular receipt was to produce some anxious enquiries from Dorothy in the next two years to her dilatory eldest brother Richard who managed the family's affairs in London. John's private profit from this voyage was less than he hoped, and he confided to William. 'Oh! I have thought of you and nothing but you; if ever of myself and my bad success it was only on your account.' The fortune that was to pay for the green field and the cow still seemed far away.

In May 1803 the *Earl of Abergavenny* sailed again to China, and if John's private trading, for which Dorothy and William again lent money, was no more successful on this second voyage, he at any rate gained some status and honour when, on the homeward voyage in February 1804 the convoy of East Indiamen came under threat from a French naval squadron waiting to intercept it off the Malay Peninsula. In an ingenious manoeuvre which made them appear to the French like armed warships, the convoy of merchant ships put the French naval force to flight after an exchange of shots. The *Abergavenny*'s log reported firing two shots at the French, but the ship was not at the centre of the action, which was sustained by the leading East Indiaman, the *Royal George*, which had her hull and sails damaged and some of her crew injured. Nevertheless John, like the other captains in the convoy, was awarded 500 guineas and a trophy of silver plate by the East India Company, and a sword by the Patriotic Fund, for his share in the successful action against the French.

Letters between Dorothy, William and John were necessarily widespread and uncertain of reaching their destination during John's two long voyages to China; and Dorothy's letters to others often mention their anxiety at not hearing from John, who was after all in danger of capture by the French during these middle years of the long Napoleonic Wars, as well as the inevitable perils of shipwreck, mutiny and piracy on the long voyages halfway round the world across wide and stormy oceans. Most of the news about John's arrivals in China and returns to England reached Dove Cottage in letters from Richard Wordsworth in London. When a letter did finally arrive there from John, it was an occasion for rejoicing and excitement among all the Dove Cottage party, including the old servant Molly Fisher, who made Dorothy promise to pass on her 'very best compliments' to her favourite, '*poor* Maister John'. Dorothy added her own affectionate message: 'We all join in best Love. Do write soon. Ever your affectionate Sister Dorothy, who wishes you many and many a happy year from the bottom of her heart.' She thought about him continually, she told him in the following year.

No letters written *en voyage* from him to her have survived, but whenever he landed in England again, he sent presents to Dove Cottage: books and a new silk hat for William, a tip for old Molly Fisher, a gown for Mary, boxes of tea for the household. His letters to Dorothy when he was in London between voyages lack the tension of the urgent words he wrote to Mary, and have no literary distinction, but they are relaxed and chatty, full of the easy solidity of a good sibling relationship, which he and Dorothy had reinforced during his 1800 visit to Grasmere. His main topics were the publication and reception of the *Lyrical Ballads* and his own reactions to them; and the family's financial problems and arrangements. Public affairs – the war with France and its effect on prices, King George III's madness – are mentioned only briefly. Meetings in London with Coleridge and the Lambs are touched on; cousins' children seen on country visits are affectionately described – John was fond of children's company. Dorothy is urged to wear thick shoes when she goes for walks in the rain, to avoid the rheumatism which he himself suffered after wearing thin shoes and silk stockings in London instead of his usual thick boots and worsted stockings, an imprudence which he deplored in terms worthy of Jane Austen's Mr Woodhouse and his anxiety over Jane Fairfax's wet stockings.

It has been suggested that after Mary's marriage to William, John deliberately avoided returning to Dove Cottage when he was on leave, though often urged to do so, but his letters do not bear this out. He often expressed to Dorothy, after as well as before the marriage, his wish that he could get back to Grasmere and see them all again. He even expressly mentioned wishing to see Mary in the gown he had sent her. But he had to stay within easy reach of the East India House and his ship.

Chapter Three

WHEN IN AUGUST 1804 John Wordsworth returned to England from his second voyage to China as captain, a voyage which had not proved as profitable as he had hoped, he spent his first months ashore in an energetic campaign to get his employers, the East India Company, to allot the *Earl of Abergavenny* to the most remunerative of the alternative routes to China when their next convoy set out. East Indiamen captains could make as much for their own account as £30,000 out of the round trip to China and back; he hoped this time to earn enough to provide a secure income for William and his family, so that William could concentrate on writing his poetry, in whose value to the world John firmly believed.

He had several strings to pull. His father's cousin, the John Wordsworth who had been the previous captain of the *Earl of Abergavenny*, and was one of the shareholders in the ship (the East India Company did not actually own the East Indiamen – they were chartered from groups of shareholders who had paid for their construction) wrote to William Dent, the principal shareholder or 'ship's husband' of the *Abergavenny*, on the younger John Wordsworth's behalf. John also wrote himself to Henry Neville, second Earl of Abergavenny, whose wife was a relation of another shareholder in the ship, Thomas Robinson, a Member of Parliament and a man of influence celebrated for his ability to get jobs for his friends and relations; he was a cousin of John's father. The ship got its name from the Abergavenny family connection.

The strongest string available for John to pull led to William Wilberforce, the crusader against the slave trade. Wilberforce had been at Cambridge with the Wordsworths' uncle William Cookson; the two men remained friends, and Cookson linked Wilberforce to his Wordsworth niece and nephews. Once when Dorothy was staying with the Cooksons at the same time as Wilberforce, she was teased by a friend who suggested that she and Wilberforce were in love. Dorothy derided this suggestion, but she was heartily interested in Wilberforce's anti-slavery campaign, and he liked her enthusiastic sympathy and gave her ten guineas for charitable donations. It is possible that a residual warmth of remembered friendship with the sister, joined with Cookson's advocacy, inclined Wilberforce to support the brother's interests sixteen years later. He introduced John to Charles Grant, Chairman of the Court of Directors of the East India

Company, who, like Wilberforce, was a member of the Evangelical group, the Clapham Sect.

The East India Company and all its activities were held in a tight network of nepotism. East India stock was often bought mainly for the patronage which it conferred, which enabled shareholders to find senior administrative posts, writerships, cadetships in India and naval commissions for their sons, brothers and nephews, though string-pulling alone was not enough – you had also to be good at your job, as John Wordsworth undoubtedly was, to get the plum posts. An example of nepotism at work in the Company's services can be seen among the ship's company and cadet passengers in the *Abergavenny*, in addition to its captain's own appointment through his relationship to the previous captain. The third mate was Joseph Wordsworth, son of John Wordsworth senior. The midshipman Benjamin Yates had a cousin in the Accountant General's department of East India House. Cosmas Stewart, a cadet passenger en route to India to join the East India Company's infantry there, was the son of the ship's purser C. H. Stewart. Two other cadet passengers, James and Robert Dent, were nephews of the 'ship's husband', William Dent.

There was nothing unusual, or peculiar to the East India Company, about this reticulation, it was the normal practice of the day in almost every institution – in the Army, the Church, the universities, as well as in commercial bodies like the East India Company. Though in some countries we now deplore nepotism, it has been the norm throughout history, and still is today in many parts of the world, where it is taken for granted as having the first call on family and tribal loyalty. John Wordsworth saw nothing ignoble in his string-pulling, though it gave him a good deal of worry. 'I cannot express the trouble and anxiety I have had upon this occasion. I have been ill and well, well and ill according as my hopes have been raised or depressed but however it has been of this service to me that I have found and made friends that are very powerful and very willing to serve me,' he confessed with guileless candour to Captain Wordsworth senior.

He regarded Wilberforce as the powerful friend who had been the most effectual in getting him the voyage he wanted. Wilberforce himself was not in particularly good odour with the East India Company, which he had seriously annoyed a few years earlier by trying to get Parliament to install schoolmasters and chaplains throughout India with the object of converting the Indians to Christianity, a project which was 'strongly reprobated' by the horrified Court of Directors of the Company. But he was a celebrated and influential figure, chief protagonist in and out of Parliament in the campaign to abolish the slave trade, friend and supporter of the Prime Minister, William Pitt. He was also, as John put it, 'the great friend and Brother Labourer in the same vineyard with Mr Grant the Chairman of the Court of Directors', the 'vineyard' being the Clapham Sect, and in John's view it was Wilberforce's influence on Grant which had been the most effective of the strings he pulled.

There were three routes to the Far East which the East India Company's ships could be ordered to take. The least remunerative of these was the voyage direct to China, which the *Abergavenny* had taken in 1801–2 and 1803–4. The other two possibilities involved calling in India en route; these were the Bombay-and-China or Bengal-and-China voyages. John hoped for one or other of these two, but preferably the Bengal one. An India House official later reported that the biggest of the Company's ships, 1200-ton vessels like the *Abergavenny*, were generally consigned to the China direct route, but 'the Company, ever attentive to commercial experiments, from their good opinion of the Commander, fixed on the *Earl of Abergavenny* to lade cotton from Bengal for the Canton market'. In fact there had been complicated manoeuvrings between John Wordsworth's supporters and other East India House notabilities who had their own candidates among the East Indiamen captains competing for the best routes, and for a time it looked as if John might get the Bombay route. But in September 1804 he was able to write triumphantly to Dorothy that he was going to get, 'far beyond my expectation', the

Bengal one. 'John is in great spirits. Through the influence of Mr Wilberforce he has got what he calls "a better voyage" that is he does not go direct to China as before' Dorothy told a friend.

The voyages via India were more profitable than the China direct one because different cargoes could be taken on and unloaded at all three stages. From England to India, the East Indiamen carried an extraordinary variety of goods for the British administrators and Army officers in India: furniture, books, cutlery, boots and shoes, enamel boxes, feathers, toys, lace, musical instruments, carriages, saddlery, glass, grocery, paint, hosiery, fishing tackle, millinery, claret, perfumery, cider, ham, ale, even packs of hounds. They also carried, very profitably, passengers: military officers, merchants, clerks, and their wives and children, going out to join the establishment in India. Passengers and much of the cargo of goods would be unloaded at Bombay or Calcutta, though some ships also carried lead, copper, tin, woollen goods and silver bullion destined to stay on board for the next port of call, the Chinese port of Canton. The *Earl of Abergavenny*'s cargo on the 1805 voyage was worth, according to the ship's manifest, just under £90,000, but subsequent newspaper reports raised this to £200,000. The cargo for Bengal included a wide variety of goods for the British community in India, but it also included chests containing silver dollars worth £70,000 to pay for goods taken on in

Bengal and China. The official cargo which East
Indiamen took on in Bengal for China usually consisted of cotton, rice, sandalwood and indigo. In
China they took on tea, silk and porcelain for the
home market in England.

But from Bengal to China they generally carried
(and John Wordsworth undoubtedly intended to carry
in the *Abergavenny* on this voyage) an unofficial
cargo, the most profitable one of all, opium. This was
made possible because East Indiamen captains had
the right to carry a considerable tonnage of cargo in
their ships for their own account, in addition to the
official cargo belonging to the Company.

The privilege, or 'indulgence', awarded by the
Company to its ships' captains to trade on their own
account was their real remuneration. Their salaries
were only £10 a month; it was the profits of private
trading, plus the passengers' fares which were also
paid to the captains, which enabled them to make
fortunes which varied between £4,000 to £12,000 per
voyage, and had sometimes reached as high as
£30,000, though also sometimes, as in John Wordsworth's previous China voyages, merely broken even
or resulted in considerable loss. John and his family
invested £20,000 of their own money in his trading
venture on this latest voyage, so access to the Bengal/
Canton opium trade was very important to him, as
the best hope for a large return on the Wordsworths'
investment. The assignment to him of the Bengal/

Canton route would enable him to take on board in Calcutta, for his own account, large amounts of cotton, rice and opium for China. The East Indiaman captain who got first to China with a cargo of Bengal opium would be able to sell it at the top of the market in Canton, and make a handsome profit.

The Chinese had been importing opium from Arab traders since the seventh century. By the end of the eighteenth century the demand had increased enormously, and was being partly met by Portuguese, Dutch, Russian and American ships carrying the inferior opium grown in Turkey. The finest opium, the Patna or 'Company's' opium, was by now grown in Bengal; its cultivation was an East India Company monopoly, inherited from the Mogul emperors. It was auctioned in mid-December every year to private owners of special opium clippers, as well as to East Indiamen captains, for the run to China; a normal cargo might be as much as 500 chests of opium, each of 160 lbs.

This was officially banned at both ends; the Company forbade East Indiamen to carry opium to China, and the Chinese Government issued many edicts against opium importation. Both authorities were aware of the malign effects of opium addiction. Successive orders from the Chinese Emperor to the Viceroy of Canton prohibited the import of the drug 'because it wasted property and destroyed the constitution'. One mandate against opium announced that, 'Vagabonds clandestinely purchase and eat it, and continually become sunk into the most stupid and besotted State, so as to cut down the power of nature, and destroy life... an injury to the minds and manners of men'. This imperial edict patronizingly suggested that the Celestial Empire did not forbid the growing and consumption of opium in foreign regions if that was the local custom, but it must not be allowed to flow into China, to corrupt the bureaucracy as well as destroying the 'vagabonds' who were addicted to it. The Imperial Government was probably more concerned about the corruption of the bureaucracy than about the fate of the 'vagabonds'; in reality Chinese officials made such huge profits out of conniving with opium importation that the Imperial edicts were largely a dead letter, in spite of their threats of dire penalties to corrupt Canton officials; 'shiver when you read this' one such edict ended menacingly.

The huge sums paid by buyers for Bengal opium when it reached the Canton market were a drain on China's supply of specie, it endangered the country's balance of trade; from the Chinese Government's perspective the import was disastrous in several ways, but quite uncontrollable. The East India Company well knew this; any protests they received from China about the opium trade were, they considered 'merely *pro forma* and without the least intention of taking any effectual steps for the suppression of a

Trade, which the Officers of the Government have so long and so notoriously found it to their interest to connive at'.

The Company's own policy about the opium trade was more complex. They too were aware of the pernicious effects of the drug. The Directors declared that 'if it were possible to prevent the use of that drug altogether except strictly for the purpose of medicine, we would gladly do it in compassion to mankind'. But if they did not supply it from Bengal, their Portuguese, Dutch and American competitors would supply it from Turkey. An outlet for the Bengal crop was essential, as its profits were needed to pay for the Company's administration in India; the cost of the Napoleonic Wars to the British Government was absorbing revenues formerly available to finance imports such as tea. If the Company could have a monopoly of opium supply to China, they might then consider reducing its production; once their trade rivals were eliminated, as sole suppliers they could then get higher prices for a reduced supply. As the Company's Council in India chillingly put it, 'the passionate fondness for it which prevails among the inhabitants of China and the Eastern tribes, would probably secure a considerable consumption at any price, and altho' the sudden deprivation of the drug would almost certainly occasion great distress to those accustomed to the use of it', there was no 'moral obligation' on the Company to regulate the supply;

reducing it would depend on whether they enjoyed a monopoly. They therefore officially forbade any opium to be laden on Company ships by captains or their officers, in accordance with the Chinese Government's ban, but continued to cultivate opium and to turn a blind eye on what happened to it after they had auctioned it in Calcutta, from where it was regularly exported to Canton by East Indiamen captains trading on their own account, and by the privately owned 'country ships'.

On both sides, the Chinese as well as the East India Company's, the factor determining policy was not ethical principle but national commercial advantage, involving connivance and deliberate oversights well understood by both sides. The danger to the health of the Chinese population was recognized, but not accepted as involving a compulsive 'moral obligation'.

Where, within this concern for national interests which cynically governed the policy of the East India Company and the Chinese Government, was the individual's conscience to place him? What did John Wordsworth feel about his privileged trading and its implications? He of course knew that in carrying opium to sell in Canton he was smuggling – breaking both his own employers' official regulations and the Chinese authorities' prohibition. But he had a relaxed attitude to smuggling where it was a recognized, though forbidden, practice. A few years earlier the

Company had fined him £210 for smuggling camlets, light cloth fabrics, to China, trade in these being restricted to the Company. Admitting that he had acted against the rules, he protested that 'it has been so constantly done for years by everyone in the service that we began to consider we had a *right* to smuggle them. We are the first that they have fined and of course we think it very hard and unjust.'

Smuggling opium would have seemed to him no more reprehensible than smuggling camlets. The smugglers' trade, which in general did no harm to individuals, and had an adventurous glamour, enjoyed a prestige and tolerance in public opinion which was not accorded to other breaches of the law, and smuggling opium carried no more stigma than smuggling brandy or French lace. Though the authorities in India and China were aware of the evil effects of opium-taking, public opinion in England at that time was not. It was regarded as a useful medicine, its addictive power was little understood, and its use was seen as no more than a personal idiosyncrasy. Two of John Wordsworth's friends, Coleridge and the much-admired Wilberforce, took it habitually. John was so little aware of the dangers of drug-taking that he was as prepared to bring hashish home from his voyages for Tom Wedgwood as he was to bring tea or dessert services, landscape prints or mandarin figures as garden ornaments, for his family and other friends.

Modern readers may find it difficult to see heroic status in a merchant navy captain who got his job partly by nepotism, was not averse to smuggling, and hoped to make his fortune by opium trading. But that would be hindsight; by the standards of his day, John Wordsworth was a man of integrity, an upright honourable citizen, respected and admired by everyone who knew him.

THE *EARL OF ABERGAVENNY* had been anchored at Gravesend while John negotiated the route for her next voyage, and when in September 1804 he secured the coveted Bengal/China route, he turned his attention to preparations for the voyage, on which he spent the rest of that autumn, based in London, at Staple Inn with his brother Richard, but frequently visiting his ship. He could not actually stay on board till the last moment, as once they had settled in on board East Indiaman captains were not allowed to sleep ashore again before the ship sailed. Moreover, he had to take a formal farewell of the Court of Directors before sailing, a ceremony for which he had to wait, as East India House postponed it from the date first agreed.

Though he might occasionally rail against the stupidity of life on board ship, or the uncertainty of seagoing plans, John was ardently proud of his ship. When he was appointed her captain in 1801 and visited her for the first time, he boasted to Mary of

be cluttered by pens and coops for the livestock carried to feed the passengers en route, but the ship as a whole had fine graceful lines, and was an object of much dignity with her towering masts and sails.

John's main task that autumn was recruiting the officers and crew for the voyage. The ship carried fourteen officers besides John, who was that autumn, at just thirty-three, among the oldest men on board. The chief mate, Samuel Baggot, was thirty; none of the other mates – W. G. E. Stewart, second mate; John's cousin Joseph Wordsworth, third mate; Thomas Gilpin, fourth mate; John Clarke, fifth mate; H. Mortimer, sixth mate – were over twenty-five, the youngest of them, John Clarke, was only nineteen. The only officer of the older generation was the purser C. H. Stewart who was fifty-four. The ship also carried a surgeon, a midshipman-coxswain and four midshipmen. In those war years, good officers were more easily come by than reliable crews, since any capable seaman was liable to be recruited by, or press-ganged into, the Royal Navy. On all his voyages as captain John had great difficulty in manning his ship; often he was tricked by seamen who had been taken on but deserted before the ship sailed. He took a poor view of the crew who embarked on the *Earl of Abergavenny* for this voyage. 'We are but very indifferently manned, our petty officers are all good men but the rest are only *trash* – tho bad as we are, I believe we are better off than any ship of the

Season. I could get men here and very good men but if I was *caught* shipping men that belonged to the Navy I should be dismissed the Service.' Scrutinizing the men available, he weeded out the steward Speke who had sailed with him before, because of his drunkenness, and considered ruling out William Akers, 'an exceeding good steady man' who had also sailed with him before but was incapacitated by a liver complaint. However in the end Akers was signed on as ship's steward. John evidently kept a careful eye on individual members of his crew.

The total number of the ship's complement was variously recorded as 160, 164 or 200, rather above the normal East Indiaman complement of 130. Most of them were English, but some were Irish or 'North Britons', and there were Americans, Danes, Russians, Prussians, Italians, Portuguese, Swiss, Germans, 'Creoles' and Chinese among them. The oldest was fifty-six, the youngest fifteen; most were in their early twenties. A total of 114 were simply seamen or ordinary seamen, but the various activities on board an East Indiaman involved a surprising variety of specialized jobs. Besides the Petty Officers – the boatswain Anthony Goham, the gunner Thomas Abbott and the carpenter John Atwater – whom John considered 'all good men', and other crew members like the armourer, sailmaker and cauterer and their mates, and the boatswain's mates, who were concerned with the ship's structure and movements, there were a dozen who were needed for the catering on a ship which carried passengers as well as crew: stewards, a butcher, a poulterer, a baker and several cooks.

While the ship lay at Gravesend, with three of the mates on board to supervise her loading, lighter after lighter brought alongside her main trading cargo: copper ingots, tin, iron, cloth, haberdashery, millinery, glass, Wedgwood pottery, books, greatcoats, horse harness, wine, beer, gun flints, and the most important item, destined to pay for opium from Bengal and tea from China: no less than 250,000 ozs of silver specie, valued at £67,000–£70,000.

They also brought a quantity of stores of food and drink for those on board during the voyage. For the crew there was beef, bread, oatmeal, herrings, rum, and lime juice to ward off the scurvy. For the passengers there were also more luxurious items: butter, coffee, potted tongue, peas, bacon, claret, brandy. All these could be loaded well in advance, but the more perishable food had to be taken on board in the crowded last days before sailing: vegetables such as carrots and turnips which might last till the ship could call at the Azores or Rio de Janeiro to take on fruit and greenstuffs, before she rounded the Cape of Good Hope; and the livestock – a cow, sheep, rabbits and hens – for which the services of the butcher and poulterer crew members would be needed, and which would be housed in the pens and hutches on top of the roundhouse.

Some idea of what the *Earl of Abergavenny*'s passengers would have expected at their dinners at the captain's table can be drawn from an East Indiaman's menu for sixteen passengers a few years earlier: it included pease soup, roast leg of mutton, hogs' puddings, two fowls, two hams, two ducks, corned round of beef, mutton pies, pork pies, mutton chops, stewed cabbage, potatoes and plum puddings, washed down by porter, beer, sherry, port, gin and rum. This lavish meal was served at two in the afternoon at the captain's table in the cuddy, on the port side of the roundhouse, and was accompanied by a good deal of ritual. The passengers wore evening dress and were seated in strict order of precedence with the two senior ladies each side of the captain, who sat in the middle of the long table facing the quarterdeck. He was expected to 'lead the conversation and exert his authority to preserve decorum . . . no debauching or late seats are ever countenanced'. After dessert and coffee, the ladies withdrew for music and conversation in each others' cabins, in which many of them kept their own cups and glasses and tea-making apparatus for sociable gatherings and private refreshment. Meanwhile the men (including the first and second mates, the surgeon and the purser, who dined at the captain's table with the passengers) remained till the port had circulated a few times; the captain then rose and said 'Good afternoon' and the men at the table were then expected to disperse.

the Fourth Mate and the midshipmen. Here too sat most of the cadet passengers who were going out to join the Company's army in India. They only actually got their commissions when they reached India, so it was very much in their interest to get there as soon as possible, and there was a rush of applications for passages on the *Abergavenny*. Both the captain's and the third mate's tables were soon fully booked, and many disappointed applicants were left behind.

The business of who sat at the captain's table was an important financial perquisite for John. An East Indiaman captain was entitled to the fares paid by passengers from England to India, as their food was provided at his expense; and the fares for the captain's table were considerable, varying according to the passenger's rank. A general would have to pay £250, a colonel or a senior merchant £200, a clerk or subaltern £110, an assistant surgeon or cadet £95. The few ladies – seldom more than four per voyage – who took passage to India might have to pay as much as £500.

The voyages for which these fares were paid were a mixture of enjoyment and considerable discomfort. The food was admirable, there were card games, dancing to the ship's band of drums and fifes, sometimes theatrical performances by the passengers. On the other hand, there were restrictions and discomforts which could cause trouble with passengers who, as a later pamphlet about the *Abergavenny*'s voyage put it, were 'most of them fully acquainted with the luxuries of life, and perhaps not blessed with the mild forbearance of their host' John Wordsworth. No fires were allowed after eight in the evening, candles in the cabins had to be put out by 10 p.m., punctual attendance at dinner was de rigueur. Ladies were not expected to play cards or backgammon, or drink more than two glasses of wine, or walk on deck unless arm in arm with another lady, and indeed they had to spend most of the voyage in their cabins.

And those cabins were no more than cubicles with canvas screens laced to the ceiling and the floor. In those years of the war at sea, space between decks had to be easily freed for the guns to be run out, so canvas curtains which could be rapidly dismantled were substituted for wooden-walled cabins. On the *Abergavenny* the canvas cabins were not even put up till after she sailed from Gravesend. They were in sections of the roundhouse and the great cabin below, and were often stuffy and dark, and anything but soundproof. Passengers on East Indiamen often complained of the unceasing racket of shouted orders and running crew on deck, of bawling children, of the lowing, bleating and crowing of the livestock over their heads on the poop. There were foul smells, too, of human and animal excrement – the ship's only latrine projected from the ship's side astern of the roundhouse – of the bilge, of rancid food from the cook's galley, of seasick and drunken vomit.

Yet these squalid cubicles were often elegantly furnished. Passengers provided their own furniture – bedding, chairs or a sofa, wash-hand stand, bookcases, hanging lamps – which would be landed with them in India to furnish their houses there. Some ladies even had harps or pianos with them in their cabins. The captain's own stateroom, which occupied the starboard side of the cuddy, next to the dining saloon, could be furnished by the more dandified East Indiaman captains with mahogany furniture, be hung with Indian chintz, and have green and gold walls, though it was unlikely that John Wordsworth – used to the newspapered walls and curtainless bed of his room at Dove Cottage, and keen to save every penny to endow his family – would have indulged in such luxuries.

The passengers for Bengal who embarked in the *Abergavenny* at Gravesend included a clerk, Archibald Grant, a Doctor Maxwell, John Routledge, described by John Wordsworth as 'as good and quiet a man as ever took passage in an Indiaman', who had a black servant with him, and twenty-six cadets on their way to join the Company's artillery, cavalry and infantry troops in India. The passengers who most interested John, and who were at least equally interested in him, were a party of three women and one man: Thomas Evans, a senior merchant in the Company's service, returning to India after home leave, accompanied by his daughter (according to

one record, his natural daughter) Emilia, his niece
Rebecca Jackson, and a widow, Margaret Blair, variously reported as 'Miss Evans's companion' and as
'proceeding to settle the affairs of her late husband'.
Probably she needed to go to India for her own affairs,
but was glad to act as duenna to the two young ladies
in return for payment of her fare.

The *Abergavenny*'s trip in a convoy of East
Indiamen from Gravesend to Portsmouth, where she
arrived on 23 January 1805, started inauspiciously.
When she left her Northfleet berth for the Downs,
the appointed pilot refused to sail because of fog,
and went ashore; when the fog cleared a replacement
pilot had to be hired. John had good reason to dis-
trust pilots from his experiences of them. When the
convoy was in the Downs there was a heavy gale
from the west and the ship collided with another East
Indiaman, the *Warren Hastings*, which had dragged
her anchor in the gale. The *Abergavenny* escaped
lightly, being struck a glancing blow on the starboard
bow which carried away part of her anchor and its
supporting beam; if it had struck the *Abergavenny*'s
bowsprit a few feet further forward, she might have
lost her masts, John considered. As it was, she did
not even lose her anchors and cables as most of the
other East Indiamen in the convoy did in the gale; 'a
most extraordinary piece of luck . . . I cannot say how
glad I am we have escaped so well,' John wrote gratefully. The *Warren Hastings* was not so fortunate, she

suffered £2,000 worth of damage to her gun and poop
decks and the necessary repairs caused her to miss
the convoy, with which it was so important to travel
if the captain was not to lose the private trading
profits available to the East Indiamen which got first
to India and China.

It was altogether a cold and uncomfortable trip
from Gravesend to Portsmouth, with snow and sleet;
everyone on board suffered from the cold, and a good
many of them, including briefly John himself, from
seasickness. But there was no let-up for the ship's
company; the carpenters were hard at work repairing
the bows after the collision (which meant that they
had no time to put up most of the canvas cabin
partitions) and the third mate, Joseph Wordsworth,
was busy with the cables on the gun deck, but this
– as John reassuringly pointed out when writing to
Joseph's father – meant that 'he did not feel so much
of the cold and Wet as some of the other officers' and
he was in fact very well.

Not so the Evans party, who were all confined to
their cabins by seasickness, but surprisingly this did
not prevent John, according to Thomas Evans, from
being 'generally with us, except when the important
duties of his station engaged his time'; he showed 'an
anxious desire to promote the comfort and happiness
of all under his protection'. John on his side enjoyed
the company of Evans and his family, who were
'moderate in their wishes and expectations and *seem*

to be pleased with *me* and the ship'. William later wrote to Thomas Evans that John 'had promised himself much happiness from the society of you and your family during the voyage'. William consoled himself with a vision of the delight which the poetry-loving John would have found in reading his favourite passages to Emilia and Rebecca. Perhaps William, with his single-minded egoism and justified confidence about his own poetic power, may have felt that John's favourite passages to read to the young ladies might have included some from William's poems, copies of which always accompanied John 'as one of the chief solaces of his long voyages' according to William.

We do not know whether John did actually find time to read aloud William's or any other poetry to the seasick girls in their cabin, but he certainly made a considerable impression on them; they were 'proud to acknowledge his kindness and attention to them'. John's appearance was prepossessing. No portrait of him exists, but William and Dorothy described him as tall and very handsome, 'a manly person, one of the finest countenances ever seen', and that this was not just the exaggeration of sibling partiality is shown by Charles Lamb remembering John's 'noble person', his cheerfulness, his 'sensible modest manly voice'. The nearest we can get to an idea of John's appearance is that Southey said that Caroline Baudouin, daughter of William Wordsworth and Annette Vallon, was 'surprisingly like John Wordsworth'. A portrait of Caroline in middle age shows a woman with a high forehead, small wide-apart eyes, a beaky nose like her father's, and a firm but humorous mouth. Her strong features would look handsome on a man's face. Perhaps some notion of what John would have looked like had he lived to middle age can be deduced from this portrait.

The East Indiamen captains had an aura of prestige. They were regarded by some of their compatriots as superior to Royal Navy officers, they were entitled to carry swords with their uniforms, they were received with a salute of thirteen guns and the guard was turned out for them if they landed at any of the Company's settlements. When Mary Hutchinson said she had no address for John when he was at Portsmouth in 1801, he teasingly reproved her: 'Do you suppose that J.W. Esq etc is not to be found in such a place as Portsmouth – if you were to see how great a man I am on board my great ship you would say that I have just cause to be offended.'

His dignified person and status were enhanced by the fine uniforms worn by the East Indiamen captains – a blue cloth coat with a black velvet collar, a buff silk lining, gold embroidery on collar and cuffs, metal buttons with the Company's crest, a black stock; a buff waistcoat and breeches, white silk stockings, buckled shoes and a cocked hat. This was the full-dress version, worn on State occasions; a modified version was worn on Sundays and when going ashore; in the blasts of snow and sleet of the voyage from Gravesend to Portsmouth John presumably wore more practical working garments. Before setting out on this voyage, John had spent £1 4s od on a new hat, four guineas on silk hose and £42 at his tailor's, paying due attention to the outward man expected of an East Indiaman captain. Altogether his was a presence to dazzle Emilia and Rebecca.

When the *Abergavenny* arrived at Portsmouth, John's chief concern was the embarkation of the King's troops and recruits for the Company's army, who were to join the ship there for the voyage to India; they were waiting for her at the Company's depot in the Isle of Wight. John expected them on board on the evening of the 24th or early on the 25th, and that there would be more than 120 of the Company's troops, which he considered too many. The muster of the army contingent taken on board at Portsmouth is less well documented and more contradictory than the crew and passenger lists. Officers apart, the King's troops consisted of a corporal and eleven troopers of the 8th Light Dragoons, a sergeant and thirteen troopers of the 24th Light Dragoons, and a sergeant, Thomas Hart, and nineteen soldiers of the 22nd Infantry Regiment. The contingent for the Company's army in India numbered 108 recruits. There is evidence that some of the troops had their wives and children with them, but there is no list of these.

By 28 January they were all embarked, but most of their officers had not yet reported to John, and he was not sure who was in command of them. He heard that a Major Otway, reported to be a 'very pleasant man', was to be in command of the King's Service contingent, but Major Loftus William Otway, who was a major in the 8th Light Dragoons, was withdrawn from the contingent for India, and his place was taken by Lieutenant Gustavus Hippisley. John considered Hippisley to be 'a very moderate sensible man and I like him much'. But Hippisley was not on board in the ship's last days; he had gone ashore in Portsmouth, together with two of the mates, Baggot and Joseph Wordsworth, Ensign Whitlow of the 22nd Foot, and one of the Company's cadets, to make some last-minute purchases, and he was left behind with them when the ship sailed. Unlike the other men left behind, Hippisley, fortunately for him, seems to have made no effort to catch up with the ship. The only King's officers who are known to have been on board the ship on her last day were Cornet Burgoyne of the 8th Light Dragoons and Ensign John Whitlow of the 22nd Foot.

The purser C. H. Stewart had left the *Abergavenny* in the Downs to return to London and collect despatches for India from East India House; from there he travelled down by land to rejoin the ship at Portsmouth, where he had arrived by the 28th.

John spent nine days at Portsmouth while the convoy waited for a favourable wind to start their voyage. He passed that week busily interviewing passengers, ordering supplies and writing letters; he found time to write hopefully to William and his youngest brother Christopher, and to send his farewell and 'kindest remembrances' to Dorothy.

Chapter Five

THE SITUATION AT Dove Cottage, when John was writing his last letter from Portsmouth to his family there on 24 January 1805, had very much changed since his visit to Grasmere five years earlier. William had married Mary Hutchinson in October 1802, and by now there were two children of the marriage. The debt owed to the Wordsworth siblings by their father's employer Lord Lonsdale had at last, after many years of procrastination, been paid to them in 1803 by his successor, and William and his family now had some financial ease and security.

The elder of the two children at Dove Cottage was now eighteen months old. Ever since his birth in 1803 his aunt Dorothy's letters had been full of descriptions of Johnny, who had been named after his sailor uncle. He was a large noble looking baby, who had a 'certain dignity and manliness about him which I have never seen in any other child', wrote his doting aunt. But even she admitted that he was a boisterous child with a passionate temper, apt to scream and roar when he was crossed, and not to be trusted alone with his little sister, of whom he was so jealous that he often hit her. He was slow in learning to talk, but by now in early 1805 he had a few words: 'pie and tates' for his favourite pie and potatoes, 'up o' knee' when he wanted to be picked up, 'hooy hooy hooy' when he saw a tree or a bird or a view that interested him. His most frequent word, first thing in the morning, all day while he tottered round the house, late at night, was 'happy'.

The second child, a daughter, had been born five months earlier, and christened Dorothy after her aunt. The name was old-fashioned, the Wordsworths agreed, but William had always promised himself that his first daughter should be called Dorothy. She was a pretty baby and her father's darling, small, lively and girlish. Dorothy often pondered which of the two cherished children she loved most, and why: the sweet merry little Dorothy, who seemed to invite protective love, or the sturdy tough Johnny, with his lazy vocabulary, his sixteen teeth, his nickname 'Anny' for her; Johnny who demanded attention and aroused pride rather than the protective instinct.

For these two children their uncle John sent a message in his last letter to his brother: 'Give my little name sake and his sister a kiss for me.'

The care of these two children by their mother and their aunt Dorothy was often shared by another aunt, Sara Hutchinson, Mary's sister, who stayed with them frequently at this time, as did other old friends. Dove Cottage had begun to seem very much over-crowded for visitors. With the children's needs and noise it sometimes sickened William and Dorothy with claustrophobia, much as they loved it, and they began to think of moving. They were now leading a more sociable, less reclusive life; they kept up a steady though guarded relationship with Mrs Coleridge and her children and the Southeys at Greta Hall; and they were in constant contact with two couples, their friends Sir George and Lady Beaumont and Thomas and Catherine Clarkson. Dorothy's frequent letters to the two wives gave wonderfully vivid pictures of daily life at Dove Cottage. There was even a suggestion that Walter Scott might visit them, though William was cautious enough to suggest that Mrs Scott could not very well be accommodated, if she accompanied her husband, in Dove Cottage with its two bedrooms and its homely way of life.

Walter Scott and William corresponded that January about their poetry; Scott sent William the just-published *Lay of the Last Minstrel* and William sent Scott *Yarrow Unvisited*. William's writing had been interrupted in the summer of 1804 by frequent visitors to Dove Cottage and the birth of little Dorothy, but in the autumn he started working hard again, and described himself as 'tolerably indus-trious'. This work was a long poem on his earlier life and the growth of his mind, which was eventually to be known as *The Prelude*. By Christmas 1804 he had completed 2,000 lines, part of Book VII and the whole of Books VIII, IX and X, out of a projected total of 10,000 or 12,000 lines. Among the tranquil woods and waters where he now lived, where the war with France seemed remote, almost unreal, he recalled and made into poetry the memories, the hopes, the disillusions of his years in France, and how his experiences there and in London had fertilized the growth of his mind. Those experiences had not in the end shaken his faith that the sovereign power of Nature working in the human spirit would reveal a pattern of eternal truth which would enable men to confront 'the heaviest sorrow earth could bring'. No such personal sorrow seemed to threaten the days of that happy and productive autumn as he worked at his long poem. In early February he confessed that his work 'advances quick or slow as the fit comes', but he still planned, or anyway hoped, to have finished it by May, and then after a break to start on a further epic work still more important to him. It was a winter of hope and achievement in his poetic career.

The only shadow over Dove Cottage that winter was anxiety about Coleridge, who had sailed for the Mediterranean in search of health in April 1804 and was now in Malta acting as Secretary to the Governor. Letters from him to his wife and the Wordsworths were made scarce and irregular by the unreliability of the post in those war years. The last that had been

heard of him was in October 1804. All through the
winter of 1804–5 William's and Dorothy's letters continually mentioned their exceeding anxiety at having
no news of him, and their hopes that by the summer
of 1805 he would have left Malta, and he and they
could meet somewhere, perhaps in the south of
England.

In spite of this anxiety, it was a winter of hopeful plans for the Wordsworths, of dreams for a still
brighter future. If they stayed on at Dove Cottage,
Coleridge and the Beaumonts would come and sit
with them on summer evenings on the mossy cushions
of the summerhouse they had made at the top of their
orchard, and Walter Scott would come to be shown
the 'more retired beauties' of the neighbourhood
which the Wordsworths knew well but the tourists
did not. If later the family moved to a larger house,
they would set up a little community of their
immediate circle: William, Mary, Dorothy, Coleridge,
Sara Hutchinson, perhaps the Clarksons and the
Beaumonts, and eventually John. Perhaps it would
be in Kent, where the climate would suit Coleridge
better than the north of England. Wherever they
settled, they would plant a grove of trees close by, to
be paid for by a present which Lady Beaumont had
given them to benefit the baby Dorothy, who was her
godchild. After much deliberation the Wordsworths
had decided that the best way to spend the money
for little Dorothy would be to plant a grove whose

trees would grow as the child grew, so that she could measure herself against them year after year; perhaps by the time she was twenty they would be tall enough to give her shelter and shade.

In such plans for a joyous future the Wordsworths spent that winter. Worries about money had largely disappeared; they were not rich, but they were secure of enough for their preferred simple way of life. By the following summer Coleridge would have come back and William would have finished his long poem; perhaps he would then go on a cruise to Norway. The horizon was bright with possibilities, unclouded by any anxieties about John. They had heard recently from him with cheerful news about his prospects. He had been due to sail immediately from Portsmouth, in convoy and by a route well known to him from several previous experiences of it. When Dorothy wrote to Mrs Clarkson on 10 February, she expected that John would have sailed from Portsmouth a week earlier, in which case he should by now have reached the Atlantic. Everything was going well, and Johnny Wordsworth spoke for the whole Grasmere household when he went about all day humming, 'Happy, happy'.

PART TWO

SINKING

Chapter Six

THE CONVOY WHICH assembled in Portsmouth in
that last week of January 1805 consisted, besides the
Earl of Abergavenny, of four other East Indiamen,
the *Royal George*, the *Henry Addington*, the *Wexford*
and the *Bombay Castle*, and two whalers. The escort
vessel was HMS *Weymouth*, a 44-gun frigate com-
manded by Captain Draper, commodore of the
convoy. Throughout that week variable winds kept
the convoy waiting; on the 24th there was a fair wind
and they expected to sail next day, but a heavy south-
easterly gale blew up, and on the 28th it was still
impossible to sail, the wind threatening to veer to the
west. HMS *Weymouth*'s log records daily signals to
the convoy to be ready for departure, but it was not
till the 30th that the ships could unmoor and move
out to Spithead. On the 31st the wind was fair enough
for the commodore to give sailing instructions for an
early morning departure next day, 1 February. Even
now there was a further delay; as the convoy ships
were weighing anchor, the *Henry Addington* collided

with HMS *Weymouth*, carrying away her driver boom and gaff and smashing her cutter. The convoy had to wait while replacements were sent out from Portsmouth Dock, and it was not until two o'clock on 2 February that they finally set sail to run through the Needles Channel. Even so, one of the convoy ships lagged behind, and the rest had to wait for her till she appeared round Cowes Point.

John Wordsworth disapproved of the commodore's instructions to take the route through the Needles Channel: 'a passage I do not like much but I hope will be attended with no accident' he wrote in a last letter from Portsmouth on the 31st. He would have preferred to be allowed to sail by himself; the convoy had after all already had two collisions, the *Warren Hastings* and *Henry Addington* accidents, but the East Indiamen were under strict orders to keep together in convoy, so John, though grumbling about this to his passenger Thomas Evans, was forced to obey.

There was more delay, after night had fallen before the whole convoy got through the Needles Channel, while the *Weymouth* lay to for her pilot to be sent ashore on a sloop which was to have collected him but had been delayed; eventually the pilot had to be put on board a boat bound for Cowes. A night of confusions and misunderstandings followed, and some newspaper reports later blamed the bad handling of the frigate, while the Admiralty tried to shift the blame on to the East India Company because of the *Henry Addington* collision. Soon after the *Weymouth* led the convoy on a south-westerly course from the Needles Rocks, she began to lose sight of all but two, then all but one, then all of the convoy ships. All that night the *Weymouth* burnt a blue light at her masthead to gather the missing ships together again, but there was no sight of them. On board the *Abergavenny* the blue lights were observed, and at first taken to be the frigate's, but afterwards mistakenly assumed to be the *Wexford*'s. As day dawned none of the East Indiamen could see any signs of the frigate, so Captain Clarke of the *Wexford*, the senior captain, automatically took over as commodore of the convoy. The previous day's fair weather had changed to a hard blow from the south and west, and the convoy made no progress, but hung about, making tacks in expectation of overtaking the frigate, but all in vain.

Meanwhile the frigate *Weymouth*, her night-signals of blue masthead lights having failed to gather the convoy, spent the next day searching vainly for them, in more or less the same stretch of sea west of the Needles where they were looking for her. It was not until nine o'clock on the morning of the 3rd that a passing ship, the *Aurora*, reported seeing the convoy sailing westward at ten the previous evening. Captain Draper, assuming that the convoy was heading west of him down the Channel, made all sail westward, hoping to catch up with his charges.

The *Weymouth* tore down the Channel all the 3rd and 4th through squalls and rainstorms, her log warily mentioning every sighting of a 'strange ship'. The Channel was a dangerous place for richly-laden British merchant ships or solitary frigates; there was an enemy waiting to pounce. Just after the convoy left Portsmouth, intelligence was received by the Naval authorities that a French squadron from Rochefort was heading for the Channel where it could intercept the convoy, so a tender was sent from Portsmouth to find the *Weymouth* and the East Indiamen and order them to return to Spithead. Later that day it was announced that as the convoy ships had not reappeared at Spithead, it was assumed that if the message had caught up with them, they had taken shelter in the port nearest to where they then were, probably Torbay.

But the message had not caught up with them, and neither the *Weymouth* nor the East Indiamen were at Torbay on 5 February. The *Weymouth* had sailed straight down the Channel for two days in pursuit, as Captain Draper apparently still believed, of the elusive convoy. On the afternoon of the 5th, with a strong gale blowing, the Lizard lights were visible four leagues to the north-north-east, and – either abandoning the convoy or still hoping to catch up with it ahead – the *Weymouth* sailed out into the

Atlantic and made for Madeira, and on to Rio de Janeiro and Madras.

Meanwhile the convoy had spent twenty-four hours at anchor or tacking off the Needles, waiting for the *Weymouth* to reappear. Finally it was decided that they had better make for the next port, hoping to find the *Weymouth* there, so they tacked westward under moderate sail, and by 3 February they were off Portland Roads, where the *Weymouth* passed south of them, believing that they were still sailing westward ahead of her down the Channel, whereas in fact she was leaving them behind her *[Plate 5]*. On that Sunday the weather was more moderate, and the confused situation was lightened for the *Abergavenny* by what seemed a fortunate event: the reappearance of two of her officers who had been left behind at Portsmouth. Samuel Baggot, the first mate, and Joseph Wordsworth, third mate, almost despaired of finding a way to catch up with the ship, but finding two other men who had been left behind, one of the Company's cadets and one of the King's army officers, Ensign Whitlow of the 22nd Foot, they clubbed together and hired an open boat in which to chase the convoy. The owner of the boat drove a hard bargain; they had to pay him forty guineas, the equivalent of more than a year's pay even for Baggot, the most senior of the party. Boatmen all along the south and south-east English coast were notorious in these years for the extortionate prices they extracted from passengers boarding East Indiamen. Four years earlier John, then waiting to sail from Portsmouth, let loose a diatribe against the rapacity of the local boatmen. 'They rise in demand according to your necessities – that is for about three miles if you are in a great hurry to get off to the ship they charge you three guineas, if in a very great hurry four, and if you must be off to the ship just as much as they like, that is from 4 to 10 guineas.'

Leaving Portland Roads the convoy spent thirty-six hours rounding Portland Bill and making westwards across Lyme Bay against a contrary wind. By the evening of the 3rd the wind had begun to blow hard again, and the *Abergavenny*'s topsails had to be reefed. Next day, Monday 4th, there were strong squally gales from the west, which fouled the mizzen topsail and made it necessary to strike the topgallant masts and get the jib boom in. The other East Indiamen of the convoy were out of sight of the *Abergavenny* that day. There was a heavy rolling sea and many of the passengers and soldiers were seasick. At ten on the morning of Tuesday 5th, in strong breezes and under cloudy skies, the rest of the convoy, apart from the frigate, came into sight again.

They were now about twelve leagues to the west of Portland, and the weather was worsening, the wind shifting to an unfavourable quarter. As there was still no sign of the *Weymouth*, Captain Clarke of the *Wexford*, as commodore of the convoy, decided that it would be best for them to return to Portland Roads to wait for better weather, and perhaps to find the *Weymouth* there. He signalled the other ships accordingly, and they set off eastward. When they were about two leagues west of Portland, the other East Indiamen picked up pilots to round Portland Bill, and ran south round the promontory for Portland Roads, where they arrived safely *[Plate 6]*.

The *Abergavenny*, being sternmost of the convoy, was the last to take on a pilot, early in the afternoon. The wind was then west-south-west. By four o'clock all hands had been called and the reefs let out, the mizzen topsail loosed and the jib boom got out, and she set off, lagging behind the rest of the convoy, to round Portland Bill as a strong ebb-tide was setting in. She was unlucky in her pilot; most later comment blamed pilot error as at least partly responsible for the event which followed. By one account he was a Portlander, hired on the strength of his local knowledge, particularly of the much-feared Shambles. But the general verdict was that he 'did not seem well acquainted with the coast'.

John had always been distrustful of pilots. William told a friend that John 'had indeed a great fear of Pilots and I have often heard him say that no situation could be imagined more distressing than that of being at the mercy of these men; oh, said he it is a joyful time for us when we get rid of them'. It was at the mercy of this unreliable man that the *Abergavenny* set off to round Portland Bill.

The light of a stormy February afternoon was fading as the ship sailed south. Away on the port side was Chesil Beach, booming as the great waves dragged its millions of pebbles grinding down in the backwash, a crashing roar so great that it could drown all other sounds near it. Hanging from the south end of Chesil Beach was the grim outline of Portland Island, a solid lump of limestone nearly 5 miles long and 2 miles wide, all but 500 feet high at its highest point but sloping almost to sea level at its southern tip, so that at some angles its shape looks like a humped dinosaur with a stretched neck; from others it seems a flattened pyramid. Treeless and bleak, crowned with ruined castles, and quarries from which the stones of Inigo Jones's Banqueting Hall and Christopher Wren's St Paul's had been dug, it was ringed with savage cliffs. Beyond its lighthouse-mounted tip, the Bill, the ferocious current of Portland Race swirled in eddies that varied from south-south-west to south-east with the ebb and flow of the tide, and sent great waves to break around the Bill in towering pinnacles of spray. When the *Abergavenny* was rounding it to the south, the breakwater enclosing Portland Roads on its eastward side, and the nearby prison, had not yet been built; what would have been visible from the ship's deck in the dimming light would have been a dark crouching mass of rock ringed with fierce crests of breaking waves.

Two miles out to sea to the south-east of Portland Bill lies a shoal of coarse sand, shingle and crushed shells, called the Shambles. It is nearly three miles long, running from east-north-east to west-south-west, six to seven fathoms deep at each end, but in the centre only eleven feet below the surface at low water. In calm weather its sinister presence is made visible by a constant rippling and roughening of the sea surface, which can be seen from the eastern cliffs of Portland Island. All around the shoal the seabed slopes steeply downwards to fourteen fathoms; the stretch of sea between it and Portland is deep enough to allow even the largest ships of those days to pass through it, and it was normal for experienced pilots who knew the coast to steer through it, whether eastbound or westbound. The alternative route, considered safer for those who did not know the coast well, was to steer a league or more south of Portland Bill and to swing round to the north-eastward of the Shambles.

This was the route that the *Abergavenny*'s pilot took, but he did not give the shoal a wide enough berth. As the ship was off the south-eastward flank of the Shambles, John asked the pilot, 'Are you sure you have your marks open?' This may have referred either to the points on shore by which the pilot was steering, or possibly to the points ('marks' in nautical idiom) on the leadline indicating the clearance in fathoms below the ship's hull. The pilot replied that he was sure. A minute or two later the wind suddenly dropped, and with the strong ebb-tide driving the ship westward, she drifted into the breakers off the shoal. Here a strong wave struck her and swung her round so that her bows were facing north, and she was driven head on onto the Shambles. As she struck at about five o'clock on that afternoon of 5 February, John Wordsworth was heard to cry, 'Oh pilot! pilot! you have ruined me.'

The wording of this lament is the strongest evidence that at this stage John did not think his ship was in danger of sinking. He was thinking of professional and financial ruin for himself, not of probable loss of life for the four hundred souls under his charge. A ship's captain who foresaw that would be more likely to have told the pilot, 'You have killed us all', not 'you have ruined *me*'; most likely, indeed, to have said nothing audible, for fear of causing panic among passengers and crew. At this stage, John and his officers considered that at worst there was every chance that the *Abergavenny*, once off the Shambles, could be beached on Weymouth Sands, only a few miles to the north, and everyone on board, the valuable cargo and the ship itself could be saved. But it was likely that her hull would be damaged by the grinding on the Shambles, and the ship would have to go into dock for repairs. Like the *Warren*

Hastings, she would miss the convoy and the advantage of getting to India and China first and reaping the first comer's large profits; the advantage for which John had negotiated so anxiously last 8 September, would be lost. There would be a Court of Enquiry into the grounding; perhaps the *Abergavenny* would not be repaired in time to sail at all that season, or no other convoy might be available. The £20,000 which the Wordsworth family had invested in this voyage for trading on his own account – which was to ensure the large profits which his previous voyages had failed to yield, and which were to secure William's, Dorothy's and his own tranquil future life in Grasmere – would be at best endangered, and at worst perhaps lost. 'Oh pilot! pilot! you have ruined me' was the cry of a man facing financial disaster, not shipwreck and death.

THE ACCOUNTS of what happened after the *Abergavenny* struck the Shambles were given in newspapers, magazines, pamphlets, anecdotes of survivors, and letters between the friends of those on board, and many of them differ as to the timing of events, orders given, the behaviour of officers, crew, passengers and soldiers. The most trustworthy accounts, on which the following chapters are mainly based, were the memorandum which Thomas Gilpin, fourth mate, wrote for the East India House, his answers to questions put to him by Charles Lamb, and a letter of condolence which he later wrote to William Wordsworth. Gilpin was an eyewitness and an experienced seaman. His memorandum and letters are plainly worded, clear and honest about what he himself had actually seen and what he had not; they record decisions but do not speculate about states of mind, and blame nobody (apart form a dry reference to 'the Pilot, if he may be so called' as being among those saved from the wreck). The facts in his memor-

hit head on, facing north, and into the deeper water north-westward towards Weymouth Bay. But the manoeuvre did not succeed; the wind had shifted unfavourably to the north-west about this time, and the ship stayed on the shoal for two and a half hours, the ebbing tide heaving her up and down, sometimes at nine fathoms, sometimes at only four and a half. Her hull repeatedly struck bottom, and the shocks were so great that it was difficult for officers and men to keep their footing on deck. According to Gilpin, guns were fired as a signal of distress from the moment she struck the Shambles, but other reports suggested that none were fired until about 6 p.m. or 6.30. This seems probable, since when the ship first struck, John and his officers considered that she could be refloated without serious damage when the tide turned, and there was therefore no imperative need for help which would warrant the firing of distress signals. But when it became clear that the pounding on the shoal had holed the hull planking immediately below the pumps, and leaks were beginning, distress signals were fired, and when there was no response, the ship fired another twenty guns, and continued firing at intervals throughout the next four hours, in the hope that boats would be launched from the shore to come to the rescue. Suggestions were to be made later that the ship could have been lightened if the guns had been thrown overboard, but Gilpin pointed out that this would have taken all hands more time than could be spared from the pumping and bailing, which were throwing overboard water which weighed more than the guns; the main chain pump could discharge a ton of water every minute.

At seven-thirty the *Abergavenny* floated off the Shambles. There were many conflicting reports of the time she spent on the shoal, and when she got off; some of them suggested that she was only on the Shambles for an hour, having struck at 3 p.m. and got off at 4 or 4.15, but Gilpin's official report stated that she got off at 7.30 after two and a half hours. The sun had now set, there was a heavy swell, the wind had now shifted to the east and increased to a strong variable gale, slackening into occasional lulls and then blowing up into vicious gusts; the tide had reached the ebb and was turning.

The leak in the ship's hull was at first thought to be manageable by pumping; the water in the hold was four feet deep while the ship was on the Shambles, and was kept at that level for some time by pumping. But the bottom was holed just below the larger chain pumps and while the carpenter was trying to repair these, the water gained so fast on the other pumps that even with a bucket chain of crew, soldiers and even passengers bailing at the fore hatchway and the scuttles, as well as the lesser pumps being kept going by heavy manning, the water gushed in so rapidly that the level with in the hold continued to rise, to ten or eleven feet.

At this point a decision was taken that the ship must be run onto Weymouth Sands and beached. The jib and foresails were set accordingly, but to little avail as the ship was now so waterlogged that she would not bear up. The helm was kept hard a starboard, but she would not answer to it because of the weight of water on board. The main and mizzen topsails were lowered, in an attempt with the remaining sails to swing the ship round and drive her towards the shore, but she was beginning to settle fast because of the water in her hold, and the sails could not keep her going at any speed. It was now evident that help was needed; more guns were fired, four lights were hoisted at the mizzen peak, and the ship's cutter was launched, with the purser Stewart, the third mate Joseph Wordsworth, and six seamen on board, to go and find the other ships in the convoy and get assistance from them or from the shore. They took with them the despatches from East India House to the Company in India, which the purser had brought down from London to Portsmouth. The two officers and six seamen reached the shore safely.

Why, if it was possible to launch the cutter at this time, were the ship's other boats not launched to take at least some of those on board to the shore? This question was put by nearly all the immediate press reports on the disaster. 'It is a circumstance hardly to

wild waves, and could carry a fair number of those on board, but it could not be got out without laying the main topsail aback, that is, getting it pressed against the mast by the headwind, and this would have so much delayed the progress of the ship shorewards, which still carried some momentum, that there would be no hope left of running her aground, and she would have gone down in deep water. In that case everyone on board, however good a swimmer, would have been drowned before they could reach the shore, whereas when the tide turned it would have run her into quite shallow water if she had been more manageable. In Gilpin's opinion she would have grounded on Weymouth Sands if she could have kept afloat for another twenty minutes. Moreover the job of launching the longboat would have taken men away from the still more vital task of pumping and bailing, and attending to the sails; and if it had been launched, the rush of those on board to get into it while it was alongside the ship might have caused it, and any of the smaller boats if they were launched, to be swamped and to sink. So the draconian decision was taken not to launch the ship's boats, but their lashings were cut so that if the ship went down they would float off instead of submerging with her, and would provide something for those thrown into the sea to hold on to – as in fact happened. All this time other ships had been seen and heard quite close by, and there was hope that if they would not respond

unlikely to reach the sloop that sent it. However, it did succeed in doing so, but with such difficulty that it was not sent back, as had been promised, to take away others remaining on board the *Abergavenny*.

The danger of such a passage in a small open boat over huge waves seemed so terrible to Mrs Blair that, in spite of entreaties, she refused to accompany her charges Emilia and Rebecca in the skiff. She felt that it must be safer to stay on board the ship, and so lost her chance of reaching the shore safely, as the Evans party and the other two passengers eventually did.

By now the water was rising so rapidly in the ship that the pumping and bailing needed the help of everyone available on board, not only the crew but the cadets, the soldiers and even their wives. The strenuous physical exertion of pumping in a wildly pitching ship, with icy water rising and dashing round the pumpers, exhausted even the strongest of them. The cadets, who were all under twenty, worked so hard that many of them fainted, which probably contributed to their low survival rate when the ship went down. Some of the troops, particularly the dragoons, pumped very well, but many of them were so incapacitated by seasickness that they were almost insensible, and no longer cared whether they lived or died. Some of the pumpers heroically continued to work, urged on by the officers in charge of the pumping operation who, according to one report, helped to keep them cheerful by handing out an allowance of grog, though it was later denied that any regular allowance had been issued.

Cornet Burgoyne claimed to have 'served each man pumping and bailing, with a dram to cheer their spirits' from his private stock of gin. If he did, it was not enough to raise the spirits of some of the seamen; they demanded more – 'Give us some grog!' – and when this was denied, they tried to break into the spirit room where the liquor was stored, as they were now sure the ship must sink and they were desperate for Dutch courage for their last hours. But the store was guarded by one of the officers with a brace of pistols, who remained there even when the ship was sinking. One seaman, imploring this officer to let him have some liquor, pointed out that 'It will be all as one an hour hence.' The officer replied, 'Be that as it may, let us die like men,' a convincingly seamanlike laconism which later press reports expanded to the more high-sounding: 'If it is God's will that we shall perish, we should die like men,' with an admonition to the sailor to go back to his duty.

Some of the subsequent reports suggested that Cornet Burgoyne had brought out some of his supplies of gin not long before the ship sank, and persuaded John Wordsworth to take two glasses of the cordial, and given the remainder of the bottle to those standing nearest. Burgoyne's own account only mentions supplying gin to the men at the pumps, but the rumour was later expanded to suggest that he had supplied a glass of liquor to every man on board, and this, combined with the story about the attack on the spirit room, was to give rise to a most unjustified but persistent rumour that when the ship went down John and everyone on board were drunk. There were conflicting accounts about the morale of passengers and crew on the *Abergavenny* in these last hours, when it had finally been announced to them that the ship could not be saved. There was no questioning about the morale of the officers; besides John, the mates Baggot and Gilpin were singled out for special praise for their courage, but all the officers were commended for their coolness and firm discipline, which ensured that there was no real insubordination or turbulence among the crew. But some reports did mention that the officers had to exert themselves to keep rebellious members of the crew to their duty (this probably referred to the attack on the spirit room) and that there was a good deal of disorder, confusion and uproar, 'general distress and agony', with passengers uttering despairing cries and prayers to God for mercy. Presumably, as in every disaster, a few people behaved heroically, a few were complaining and cowardly and tried to save themselves regardless of others, and the majority did what they were told, or did nothing.

It was now between ten and eleven on a pitch-black night, and the last cast of the lead showed eleven fathoms. Pumping still went on, but the orlop, the lower deck, was now full of water, and though the tide was now turning, and the north-easterly gale blowing in furious gusts, the sails of the waterlogged ship would not carry her on towards the shore, still nearly two miles away. No help had come to her either from the shore or from the other ships within reach, since the little skiff from a nearby sloop had taken off five of the passengers. The remaining passengers and crew now knew that there was no hope of the ship being saved, and her formal sentence of death was announced by the chief mate Samuel Baggot, who went to his captain where he stood on the poop and said, 'We have done all we can, Sir – she will sink in a moment.' John answered, 'It cannot be helped. God's will be done.'

These were not John's last words. In the following moments he was seen talking with 'apparent cheerfulness' to Baggot. Gilpin heard him giving orders with firmness, and the midshipman Yates heard him, shortly before the ship sank, give a shouted order to haul on board the main tack. Yates considered that this manoeuvre, hauling in the lower forward corner of the mainsail, hurried the ship down by pressing the sail against the mast. This young midshipman was, as his subsequent correspondence with Charles Lamb shows, perhaps over-confident in his own judgement and seamanship; Lamb drily suggested to William Wordsworth that he could decide for himself

how much to believe of 'this young seaman's surmises'.

Though John's answer to Baggot's warning was
not his last utterance, it became famous, figuring,
often with elaborations and suggestions, as the centre-
piece of every later account of the wreck. But who
was the source of this celebrated anecdote of what
the two men said to each other at that crisis? It cannot
have been either of them who revealed it to posterity.
Nor can it have been the second mate, W. G. E.
Stewart, who when later interviewed cautiously said
that he was in another part of the ship when she
was sinking, and could not give evidence as to what
had passed. The most likely source of the anecdote
was that it came from one of the six survivors who
are known to have been standing nearest to John
when the ship went down shortly after the exchange
between him and Baggot, and were the most likely
to have heard it. These were the coxswain William
White, a seaman called William Webber, the cadet
Robert Gramshaw, Benjamin Yates, Thomas Gilpin
and Cornet Burgoyne (who claimed that he had only
heard John say, 'It cannot be helped'; no mention of
'God's will').

At the moment of sinking John was standing on
top of a hen-coop in the forepart of the poop, between
the mizzen mast and the starboard side ladder leading
to the quarterdeck. The seaman Webber was close to
him on the poop. Gramshaw, who had gone below

to his cabin to collect his valuables, came on deck and was trying to get up the starboard ladder to the poop. Yates was in the starboard rigging of the mizzen mast, close above John, as was Gilpin, who since the strike on the Shambles had been on the gun deck organizing the soldiers working on the pumps; he only came on deck shortly before the end. Yates shouted to John to join them in the rigging, but could not hear his reply above the screams of those below them on the deck.

The ship was then quite full of water from the mainmast forwards. A heavy swell gave her an upward heave, a sudden gust of wind laid her almost sideways on her beam ends, and then another huge wave rolled over her bows, forcing them down so that the ship sank head foremost, and then rushed the whole length of the ship to the stern, carrying away everyone and everything in its path. The heavy weight of the cargo of specie and pottery made the ship settle eleven fathoms down on an even keel on the seabed, with her masts still sticking out above the surface.

Webber said that he had seen John washed off the poop into the sea. Yates, who was in the rigging on the mast which was still above the wash of the waves, was puzzled as to why John was not saved, as he did not believe that John was sucked down by the eddy made by the ship sinking. Gilpin, though he had seen John standing on the poop just before the ship sank, did not see him at the actual moment of sinking, and could not say whether he was then still standing on the hen-coop on the poop. But Gilpin's is the crucial account of John's last moments, given in a letter to William which, though sprinkled with spelling and grammatical mistakes, is grippingly vivid.

> I don't think he was wash'd overboard. I see him on the Poop, less than a minute before she went down. In the act of her going down I ran to the Poop, looking out which way to save myself, and she sinking so rapidly that as I ascended the Mizzen Shroud the water catch'd me, before I cd get up the into the top. Sum minutes after this I see several men hanging by ropes, fast to the mizzen mast amongst which was Capt. Wordsworth. I went down into the Mizzen Rigging to see if I cd render them any assistance, I got within 10 or 12 Feet of where he was, I hailed him as loud as I cd and threw him a rope, he was motionless and insensible he did not katch the rope or answer.

For almost another five minutes Gilpin saw him tossing in the waves, until he was swept away and seen no more.

~~~

THE QUESTION of whether John tried to save himself was to cause much debate. All the first newspaper reports suggested that he did not seem to want to survive the loss of his ship, and made no effort to save his life, in spite of Gilpin's attempts to get him to hold on to a rope. The first of three pamphlets about the wreck, published a few days after the sinking, included a fanciful description of John's depression before the ship sailed from Portsmouth, his 'heart-broken' demeanour when she was sinking, and his 'disdaining' to survive the loss of his ship. All of this was second-hand rumour, collected by newspaper reporters from survivors. Of the immediate eyewitnesses: Gilpin was fairly sure that John had tried to save himself; Webber, White and Gramshaw gave no opinion and Yates said he was quite certain in his own mind that John did not want to survive the loss of his property. A second more reliable pamphlet about the wreck, emanating from the East India House and published a little later than the first crop of accounts, claimed that John's manner had been calm and cheerful to the last, and that the story about his depression had no foundation.

The controversy was to last for many years. It can be encapsulated by the comments of two celebrated writers, Charles Lamb and Thomas de Quincey, a generation apart. Lamb was a friend of John's as well as of William's. De Quincey was too young to have met John, but he knew William, Dorothy and Mary well. Lamb wrote to William, when he had read the newspaper reports and discussed the story with East India House colleagues, but had not yet seen Gilpin and had his eyewitness description of the last minutes of John's life. Lamb's verdict was an open one:

> All accounts agree that just before the vessel going down, your brother seemed like one overwhelmed with the situation, and careless of his own safety. Perhaps he might have saved himself; but a Captain who in such circumstances does all he can for his ship and nothing for himself, is the noblest idea . . . The universal sentiment is, that your brother did all that duty required: and if he had been more alive to the feelings of those distant ones whom he loved, he would have been at that time a less admirable object; less to be exulted in by them: for his character is high with all that I have heard speak of him, and no reproach can fix on him.

Thirty-four years later, Thomas de Quincey was to write:

> Captain Wordsworth might have saved his own life; but the perfect loyalty of his nature to the claims upon him, that sublime fidelity to duty which is so often found among men of his profession, kept him to the last upon the wreck; and after *that*, it is probable that the almost total wreck of his own fortunes . . . but still more the total ruin of the new and splendid Indiaman confided to his care, had so much dejected his spirits that he was not in a condition for making such efforts as, under a more hopeful prospect, he might have been able to make.

Even to the very end, John Wordsworth and his quiet manner still puzzled his fellow men, who speculated and contradicted each other as they tried to solve the enigma. Was he suffering from depression which had already given foreboding signs before he sailed? Was he silent, motionless, stupefied, even perhaps drunk, in those last moments? Or was he calm, communicative, in control to the end? Did he, strong swimmer as he was, let himself drown in the waves in which other men from the ship were able to stay afloat? Or did he try to catch the rope thrown to him, but was so much weakened by the icy chill of the sea and the weight of his sodden clothes that he could not keep his hold? The stereotypical behaviour of a bluff sea captain in his situation would have been bawled orders, violent striding to and fro, perhaps a heroic arms-folded posture to indicate that he would go down with his ship. But John's attitude in these last minutes did not fit any stereotype. He remained standing on his hen-coop, making the necessary decisions, 'giving orders with all possible calmness'. Even the admiring passenger Thomas Evans (who had left the ship hours earlier) could only guess at John's state of mind and how it might seem to others; in his letter of condolence to William, he tentatively suggested that 'it may be conceived that the mild and reflecting character of your Brother was not so well calculated for the scenes he had to encounter as others who had less feeling which imposes the appearance

1. *The Earl of Abergavenny, East Indiaman,* by T. Lury

2. Dove Cottage, c. 1805, by Amos Green

7. *Sketch of a Wreck*, J. M. W. Turner. The *Abergavenny* similarly rolled over on her port side when a strong wave drove her onto the Shambles.

8. *Loss of the Abergavenny, East Indiaman, off the Isle of Portland*, by R. Cobbold and J. Thomlinson. The rescue of the men in the rigging of the half-submerged *Abergavenny*.

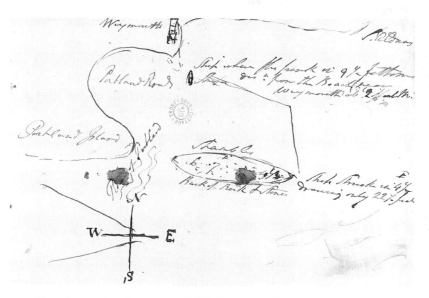

9. Sketch map by the purser, C. H. Stewart, who survived the wreck, showing the route of the *Abergavenny* in her last hours

10. Churchyard of All Saints Church, Wyke Regis, where John Wordsworth was buried

16. Samuel Taylor Coleridge, 1811: sketch after George Dawe

Chapter Eight

WHEN THE PASSENGERS and crew of the *Aber-gavenny* were told that she was sinking and that there was no hope of her reaching the shore, some of them seized loose planks, spars, pieces of coops and pens, and threw themselves into the sea. One of these was John Forbes, one of the Company's cadets on board, who was a strong swimmer; he stripped off his coat and dived into the icy waves, followed by three private soldiers. All four were picked up by a nearby boat, and stowed in its hold for fear that the boat would upset if too many men remained on deck. Another was the midshipman and coxswain William White. Though he could not swim, he threw himself into the water when he saw the ship was sinking, 'trusting for his safety, to his own active exertions, assisted by God' as he rather smugly related afterwards.

> I drifted some way from the ship on a hen-coop, with two others, when it upset and they found a

> watery grave! I tried to regain my seat on the
> hen-coop, but without effect; and in making, as I
> thought, my last effort, caught hold of a part of the
> wreck, from which a poor fellow had just lost his
> hold, and was drowned. Thank God! I at last
> regained the mizzen-rigging, almost water-logged,
> and crawled with several others into the mizzen-
> top.

It does not sound as if he had tried very hard to help
the other 'poor fellows' who had been clinging to the
hen-coop and the wreckage, but he did report that
William Akers, the ship's steward, Thomas Abbott
the gunner, and John Atwater the carpenter, had
saved themselves in the same way.

These men had all thrown themselves into the sea
before the ship actually sank. Several others besides
the captain were swept into the sea by the huge wave
which travelled along the deck from bows to stern
and sent the ship down head foremost. As well
as clearing off all the men on the deck, the wave
dislodged into the sea the longboat, whose lashings
had previously been cut, and every loose object on
the deck that would float, including the hen-coops
and the cattle-pens. The seaman Webber, who was
standing by John on the poop when the ship went
down, was washed overboard and swam for a little
time till he saw the cattle-pen floating, and scrambling
onto it found himself in the company of a cow and
some sheep, and there kept afloat till he was taken

off by a nearby boat. Besides John Thwaites, only four of the cadets who were still in the ship when she went down survived. Swept into the sea, Thwaites managed with about twenty other men to clamber into a floating boat, probably the longboat. A few yards away from the ship it upset, and all the other men were drowned, but Thwaites clung to the upturned boat, and was eventually picked up by a nearby boat 'when just sinking with fatigue and apprehension'.

Various vessels nearby did pick up Cadet Forbes and three soldiers, Webber, Thwaites and probably others; the sloop that rescued Forbes also nearly saved twelve men who were seen clinging to a spar, but at that moment a squall hit the sloop and laid her on her beam ends on top of the spar, sending the twelve men under to drown. It remains mysterious why the many ships and boats which were seen and heard to be near the sinking *Abergavenny* did not render more, and earlier, help. Some of them remained unaware of her plight because the roar of the gale drowned the noise of her guns firing distress signals. This was certainly true of the other East Indiamen of the convoy which were at anchor in Portland Roads; one of those on board these ships explained that owing to the very stormy night the firing from the *Abergavenny* was never heard, and no news of her tragedy reached them till next morning. But there were plenty of sloops and fishing vessels in the area between the

Shambles and Weymouth Bay, near enough so that they must have seen the *Abergavenny* and heard not only her distress signals but the hailing and cries of the men on board her, and more sinister motives were attributed to the failure to help her. At best, they might have been concentrating on picking up men from the sea. They were perhaps, it was suggested, afraid that if they came alongside the sinking ship there would be a rush of the men on board to jump into the boats to save themselves, and this would overload and sink the boats. The most callous motive attributed to those in the nearby boats was that they were bent on plunder, on picking up wreckage rather than men.

Cornet Burgoyne, who was one of the survivors in the riggings, recorded that when he had hailed two sloops which passed by the stern of the *Abergavenny* shortly after she sank, they answered that they would come back and pick up the men in the riggings, but they did not come back immediately as they were, 'more humanely' as Burgoyne allowed, occupied in picking up men who were in the sea clinging to pieces of the wreck. But evidence was given at the subsequent East India House enquiry by the carpenter and another seaman that as they were in the water clinging to a turkey coop, they hailed a sloop to pick them up, but were told, 'Hold fast until daylight and then you will be picked up.' Several masters of sloops were examined at the enquiry, but there was no evidence that they were responsible for this callous reply which, thought Burgoyne, 'no-one would be so inhuman as to give'. But he added that 'if the brute is found, he will certainly be severely punished'.

The most graphic description of what it was like to be washed off the sinking ship into the sea was given by a passenger, the cavalry cadet Robert Michael Oginski Gramshaw. When the crew and passengers were told that the ship must sink, he went below to his cabin with two other cadets, where they stayed for a time without speaking, distractedly looking at each other and wondering what to do to save their lives. Eventually one of the other cadets said 'let us return upon deck', and two of them did so, but Gramshaw stayed behind and collected from his writing desk his watch, his army commission, some letters of introduction and twenty guineas. He then followed the others up to the deck, but could see no sign of them. As he was standing at the foot of the steps leading up from the quarterdeck to the poop, he looked over his shoulder and saw the giant wave rushing along the deck towards him in what he called an 'immense column', and it flung him into the sea as it forced the ship down headforemost.

Gramshaw could not swim, and he was encumbered by a greatcoat and boots. The night was pitch dark, the sea raging, the gale blowing in violent gusts.

When the ship's stern went under, he was drawn round it by the vortex of her sinking and found himself on the opposite side from the one off which he had been flung. As he struggled in the sea, something dashed several times against the back of his hand, and he realized it was a rope hanging from the mizzen mast. He managed to catch hold of it, and climbed up it several feet, but the weight of his saturated coat and boots dragged him down, and he slipped from the rope into the sea again. 'His spirits now failed him, having made his utmost effort to preserve life; when, at this fearful moment, resigning himself to the will of his Creator, the ship gave a lurch, by which he was canted into the mizzen shrouds.' He secured himself as well as he could by gripping the ratlings, the ropes across the shrouds which made the ladders up the riggings. Here he remained for some time, shivering and benumbed. He was eventually spotted by Gilpin, who by now was in the mizzen top with about twenty others. He came climbing down and lifted Gramshaw up to the mizzen top and put him among the others already there.

Gilpin, who throughout that grim night showed exemplary leadership and did his best to save as many men as possible, was one of those already in the shrouds when the ship went down. With him in the first half-hour or so after the ship sank were Yates, Burgoyne, the cadet William Baillie, Sergeant Hart of the 22nd Foot, and perhaps as many as a hundred and eighty men including those like White, Gram-shaw, Abbott, Akers, and Atwater who were washed back into the riggings from the sea. Cornet Burgoyne described how he had escaped by climbing up the rigging when the ship was about to sink.

> It was then time to think of saving one's life . . . Just as she was going down, I observed the boat on the quarter was full of men, so that I was sure their lives were in danger. I therefore did not attempt to get into her, but asked the Pilot (who was then on the poop) What water there was? – he replied eleven fathoms; I then thought it possible to save myself in the tops, I therefore ran up the riggings and so preserved my life.

According to Gilpin, the *Abergavenny* went down at 11 p.m. Burgoyne thought it was a little after 10 p.m. A watch found in the fob pocket of one of the corpses later washed ashore was found to have stopped at 10.05 p.m., from which it was concluded in some accounts that the ship had gone down then, but the corpse (probably one of the passengers or officers who drowned, as they would be the most likely to have a watch and watch-fob) could have been one of those who plunged into the sea before the ship sank.

When she first settled on the sea bottom, the main and mizzen masts still remained above water to below their yards, and it is possible that as many as two hundred men were able to cling to them. But as the ship gradually settled deeper into the sandy seabed in the next hour, the men lower down in the shrouds, constantly drenched by icy spray breaking over them and benumbed by the frosty wind, lost their hold and dropped into the water below, or were washed off their precarious perches. Only those of them, about eighty or ninety, who were in the main and mizzen tops were able to cling on, wrapping themselves in the sagging sails to keep out the cold, which was so bitter that many of those in the tops were frostbitten as well as severely bruised. But they were safe there from being washed off by the waves. The only chance of survival was in getting as high as possible in the shrouds, and a struggle for self-preservation began. One of the crew, a Yorkshireman, having got himself up nearly to a safe height, was held back by one of his mess-mates seizing him by the leg. The Yorkshireman unclasped his knife and, in spite of the entreaties of the man grasping his leg, slashed at his fingers so that he fell to his death. This grisly story was told by Cadet Baillie, who was one of the earliest to climb into the shrouds; he and Cornet Burgoyne reported another horrible incident. Among those high up in the shrouds were Sergeant Hart and his wife side by side, but she lost her hold, and sliding down past him, tried in vain to stop herself by biting his arm and hand, which she lacerated. Sergeant Hart is known to have lost a wife and child in the wreck. If his wife was beside him in the shrouds with a baby in her arms, she is more likely to have lost her grip and slipped downwards, making a last desperate effort with her mouth to save herself and her child; and the wound on her husband's arm which she inflicted could explain why Sergeant Hart was the only man in the shrouds to be unconscious when rescue came. Loss of blood from his wounded arm, and the horror of losing his wife and child in this way, on top of the bitter cold and exhaustion from which all the men in the shrouds were suffering, would explain why his condition was worse than theirs.

There were incidents of courage and energy as well as of callous self-preservation and wild desperation during those two hours around midnight. Throughout the ordeal, Gilpin did his best to encourage everyone, and Burgoyne decided about midnight to try and raise everyone's morale by starting a song, and soon got the surviving passengers and crew in the shrouds to join in. This, though successful in keeping up their spirits, possibly had one unfortunate effect; some of the crews of the nearby sloops, hearing the singing, thought it 'inappropriate-seeming merriment' which meant that the men clinging to the masts were desperate and probably drunk, and would make a wild scramble onto any rescue boats, which might sink them, so the sloops held off. This sounds like an excuse; during those hours several of the sloops had been heard beating against the waves and seen passing so close to the *Abergavenny* that they must have heard the men on her masts hailing them for help, as well as singing. One of the sloops was towing two boats astern, which could have been used to come alongside the wreck and rescue the survivors, but when hailed by them, she sheered off.

Help came at last, probably at about 2 a.m. on the morning of 6 February, though some accounts put the rescue at midnight and some, improbably, as late as 7 a.m. By then there were about seventy men still clinging on in the shrouds. A sloop, the *Three Brothers*, which had heard the *Abergavenny*'s distress signals, appeared and anchored close to the sunken ship. Its boat was manned and came alongside the wreck's masts and rigging which were above the water. The weather had somewhat moderated, and the boat was able to take off the survivors, about twenty at a time, in three trips, and put them on the sloop. Fears that the survivors would rush any rescuing boats in a dangerous *sauve-qui-peut* were shown to be quite unjustified; the men climbed down from the riggings into the boat one by one, in disciplined order, as their names were called by the officers. When it was thought that everyone had got off the shrouds and the boat was about to return to the sloop with the last load of survivors, it was seen that one man was still in one of the mast tops. He was hailed, but did not answer, so Gilpin climbed back onto the wreck and up to the man, who proved to be unconscious with cold and exhaustion. Gilpin carried him down on his back and got him into the boat.

There is some confusion about this incident; it was at first said that the man was an unnamed surgeon, and that it was Mortimer, the sixth mate, not Gilpin, who carried him down, but the general consensus was that the man was Sergeant Hart, and that it was Gilpin who rescued him.

When all the survivors from the shrouds were on board the sloop, she weighed anchor and scudded with all the sail she could carry for Weymouth, with the wind now in a favourable quarter. She had not got far when Baggot, the first mate, was seen to be floating in the sea close astern. After he had told John the ship must sink, and continued talking to him for some minutes, he had been seen by Gilpin jumping down onto the quarterdeck, having told the midshipmen to take care of themselves, but Gilpin saw no more of him after the ship went down. He had managed to keep himself up in the freezing sea for at least two hours since the *Abergavenny* went down. The sloop immediately lay to when he was seen in the water, so that he could be picked up, and a rope was thrown to him which he caught, and he was about to be hauled on board when he saw that Mrs Blair was floating some distance away. She had refused to escape in the skiff which had taken off the rest of her party, because she thought she would be safer in the ship, but had been washed into the sea when the ship sank, and had somehow survived since then, presumably clinging to some wreckage. Baggot decided to try and reach her; he let go of the rope, plunged back into the sea, and swam towards Mrs Blair. He reached her, took hold of her and swam back towards the sloop, holding her head above water. Just as he had nearly reached the sloop, a great wave hit them, sending them under, and neither of them came to the surface again.

Even among the rescued there were some who were later to die of hypothermia and exhaustion on reaching land. Sergeant Hart, unconscious when he was carried down from the shrouds, was apparently dead when the survivors were landed in Weymouth. He was carried to the Globe public house, and given artificial respiration by a local surgeon called Bryers, which revived Hart enough to open his eyes and swallow some wine, but he died about twelve hours after he was landed. Cadet John Forbes had been picked up by a fishing boat and crammed into its hold with three others, but all four were so 'sad and benumbed' that they died on coming ashore though they were given first aid the moment they were landed. All the rescued men were landed at daylight and taken to the Town Hall where they were given clothes, food and grog, donated by Weymouth inhabitants, and had their cuts and bruises dressed and medicines administered gratis by Dr Bryers. Most of the survivors from the riggings recovered, but there was one other piteous case. An unnamed old Portuguese seaman was carried ashore, helpless and feverous, and put to bed in lodgings in Weymouth. He was visited by Dr Bryers, and he appeared during the next few days to be recovering. But on Saturday the 9th he asked the nurse to get a large wax candle, which he paid for with the only shilling he possessed, to light it and put it by his bedside, and not to extinguish it until he was dead. From this time, though he remained conscious and sensible, he refused all food and medicine, and would not speak, but lay with his eyes fixed on a Catholic missal, until Sunday morning when he died.

On the morning of 6 February the compiling of lists of the drowned and the saved from the wreck was begun. The first estimate, and the one generally mentioned in later accounts, was that of the 402 souls on board the *Abergavenny* when she hit the Shambles, 300 had perished. This was so generally believed that when my great-grandfather John Henry Slessor landed in Portsmouth from Jersey with his detachment of Reserve troops six weeks later, on 27 March, he found that Portsmouth was still full of talk and rumours about the wreck, and he noted laconically in his diary: 'An Indiaman lost in the Bay of Weymouth; 300 souls perished.' It was as long an entry in his diary as he accorded to the Battle of Trafalgar seven months later; he had a family interest in the event as his brother William was a Company cadet who had sailed for India nine months earlier.

When the numbers on board the *Abergavenny* were rechecked, it turned out that some of the King's troops and the Company's recruits who were thought to have been drowned were afterwards found to have escaped, and the later and more accurate lists indicate that the total number of the dead was about 260. It was a grim toll of lives, most of them young, snatched away. Besides John Wordsworth there were frightened obstinate Margaret Blair; self-sacrificing Samuel Baggot; the resolute strong swimmer John Forbes, who perished though non-swimmers survived; Sergeant Hart and his wife and baby; Ensign Whitlow, who had made such desperate efforts, when he was left behind with Baggot and Joseph Wordsworth at Portsmouth, to catch up with the doomed ship; Dun Mahomed, the black servant of Mr Routledge; the midshipman Richard Savage, the assistant surgeon Henry Durant, the boatswain Anthony Goham; nineteen cadets, weakened by their exertions at the pumps – among them the Dent brothers and Pynsent Lane, whose grieving family mourned his 'affectionate disposition and engaging manners' in an obituary note; seventeen Chinese seamen on their way home to a country they were never to see again; passengers, dragoons, Company's recruits, armourers, stewards, sailmakers, cooks and the Portuguese seaman, rescued and brought to land in vain, dying with his shilling candle burning beside him.

PART THREE

SALVAGE

Chapter Nine

THE COURT OF DIRECTORS of the East India Company met to conduct its affairs at least once a week, on a Wednesday, at its headquarters, East India House in Leadenhall Street. The building had been reconstructed only six years earlier, and now had an imposing classical façade 200 feet wide and 60 feet high, with a portico of six fluted Ionic columns supporting a pediment crowded with statues emblematic of Commerce, Navigation, Britannia, Liberty, Order, Religion, Justice, Industry and Integrity, presided over by a portly George III. The interior, however, or at any rate those parts of it to which the junior staff like Charles Lamb were relegated, was less impressive; the upper part of the building was a labyrinth of long narrow corridors, dark staircases and rooms so gloomy that for half the year the clerks had to write by candlelight all day.

Here in the Directors' Court Room on the ground floor, the directors gathered round an enormous horseshoe table on Wednesday 6 February 1805. Before the Court were letters written a few days earlier from the captains of all the East Indiamen in the convoy, including John Wordsworth, enclosing lists of the ships' companies and passengers. The normal deduction from these letters would be that by now the convoy would have passed down the Channel into the Atlantic. But some communications just received contained less satisfactory news. The Admiralty reported that Captain Draper in HMS *Weymouth* had not kept in touch with the convoy he was supposed to be escorting, and hinted that this was because the East Indiaman *Henry Addington* had collided with the *Weymouth*. A letter which must have been written on the previous evening had also just arrived from Captain Clarke of the *Wexford* to say that the convoy had been forced by contrary winds into Portland Roads, and all the East Indiamen were now at anchor there, with the exception of the *Earl of Abergavenny*.

At six o'clock on the morning of 7 February C. H. Stewart, the purser of the *Abergavenny*, arrived at the door of East India House. Having been sent ashore from the ship before she sank, he had stayed in Weymouth long enough to get some estimate of the number who had survived the wreck, and had then been sent to London to bring news of the disaster to East India House. With him was the cadet Charles Taylor, who had come ashore with the Evans party when they were rescued by a passing sloop. The news they brought was given at once to Ramsay, Secretary to the Court of Directors, who lived next door to East India House. Stewart and Taylor were soon closeted with him, but not before rumours had begun to spread that most of the *Abergavenny*'s crew and passengers had been drowned. Crowds of anxious relatives and friends, followed by newspaper reporters, began to assemble outside East India House, and even got inside its main entrance into the central corridor which ran through the building from front to back, to question the survivors and collect their 'tales of misery', as more of them began to arrive from Weymouth to report to the Company. East India House later denied that any of the crowd had forced their way in and blocked the corridor, or that any of the survivors had told tales of misery to the crowds and the reporters. But the details and anecdotes of the wreck which appeared in lengthy columns in next day's newspapers, exaggerated as they might be, can only have originated from this source. *The Times* and the *St James's Chronicle* actually claimed that an officer was the source of their accounts.

By nine in the morning, when Fourth Mate Gilpin arrived in his turn to report to the Company, he had to force his way through the crowded passages, past a barrage of enquiries, to which he seems to have supplied some answers (he is the most likely source for the story of John Wordsworth saying 'God's will be done' which appeared in most of the newspaper accounts) before he joined Stewart and Taylor in the conference with Secretary Ramsay. At eleven o'clock Cornet Burgoyne also arrived, and, though said to be 'very much fatigued', was conducted to Ramsay's office to add his evidence to that of Stewart, Taylor and Gilpin.

Rumours continued to circulate among the waiting crowds that 300 of the 400 souls on board the *Abergavenny* had drowned. It was not until two in the afternoon that Ramsay emerged and made a public statement about the disaster, including a list of the passengers and crew who had been saved, as far as Stewart and the others had been able to ascertain before they left Weymouth.

Stewart had been under cross-examination in Ramsay's office from six in the morning until two in the afternoon. He was a man of fifty-four, by far the oldest of the *Abergavenny*'s officers, and one of the oldest of the whole ship's company. He had come ashore from the endangered ship in a small boat through a stormy sea and icy winds on the evening of the 5th to seek help. He had spent that night waiting for news of the ship, hearing the dreadful news of her demise from the survivors as they were brought ashore, and then compiling lists of the saved and the missing, before posting up to London through the night of the 6th, to bring the news to East India House at dawn on the 7th. Thirty-six hours so spent would in any case have been a severe test for a man of his age, but he had a far worse anxiety to bear; not only did he know that his captain and many of his shipmates were lost, but his own son, the cadet Cosmas Stewart, was not among the survivors who had been brought ashore before he left Weymouth. When he was at last released from his long interview with Ramsay, his exhaustion and anxiety brought on him what was described as a 'strong fit', presumably a stroke or heart attack which made him unconscious. Undressed and put into a warm bed, he soon recovered consciousness, but it was to confront the knowledge that only five of the twenty-six cadets on board the *Abergavenny* were known to have survived, and that the name of Cosmas Stewart was not on that list of five.

Not all the survivors made for East India House or spent the day telling their stories to reporters. A Weymouth diarist disapprovingly recorded, as an instance of the thoughtlessness of seagoing men used to danger, that one of the quartermasters who escaped from the wreck, when he arrived in London, 'was one of the noisiest in the front row of the pit of Drury Lane Theatre' instead of going to church to return thanks for his deliverance.

Next day, 8 February, the Court of Directors met again to hear the news of the wreck from the reports of the surviving officers who had come to London; from Captain Clarke of the *Wexford* in Portland Roads, who had by now heard what had happened to the *Abergavenny*; and from various individuals and firms who were already ghoulishly applying for the job of salvaging the ship. The Court's minutes, which did not indulge in expressions of feeling, coldly made their first reference to the disaster by recording the receipt of these communications 'relative to the loss of the Earl of Abergavenny'.

The newspapers, however were not so restrained. On 8 February the *Times*, the *Courier*, the *Morning Herald*, the *Morning Chronicle*, all published lengthy reports about the shipwreck. It is rather surprising that the London newspapers should have given such detailed coverage to the story of a civilian shipwreck at a critical moment in the Napoleonic Wars when they were also daily reporting the movements, chases, escapes, sinkings of Royal Navy ships in encounters with enemy French ships. Napoleon's 'Army of England' was encamped on the cliffs of Boulogne, ready to be shipped across the Channel to invade Britain as soon as the French ships of the line based on Brest, Rochefort and Toulon could elude the vigilance of the British Navy and hold the Channel long enough. In February 1805 Nelson was still holding the Toulon fleet bottled up, and British warships were keeping a watch on Brest and continually beating up and down the Channel to frustrate the enemy's intentions. That the loss of the *Abergavenny* was still headline news was due perhaps to the very high loss of life when she sank, and of her exceptionally costly

to give much pain to the families of the drowned, and which remained entwined with the history of the wreck for years to come. Some of the errors were obvious and easily refuted. Both the *Courier* and the *Morning Herald* said that John Wordsworth had left a wife and a large family of children. It was suggested that the ship's boats were not launched to take the passengers and crew to safety because this was 'forgotten' in the hurry and confusion; the publication of Gilpin's memorandum proved that the decision not to launch the boats was a deliberate choice as the lesser of two evils. John was said to have been in such a state of depression before the ship sailed that he could not face the customary ceremony of taking leave of the Court of Directors, which therefore had to be postponed; the East India House refuted this by pointing out that the postponement was not at John's instance but was because the necessary formalities had not been completed. (Both the rumour that he had been uncharacteristically depressed before the *Abergavenny* sailed, and a contradictory report that he was 'so elated with the hopes of a prosperous voyage that his friends professed a concern at his unusual flow of spirits' had an unsensational foundation of truth. He himself said that he had been alternately well and ill as his hopes of getting the Bengal–China route had been raised or depressed.) Another incorrect report was that he had never spoken again after his 'God's will' exchange with Baggot; eyewitnesses on board were able to show that he later talked cheerfully to Baggot, and gave orders about the sails.

More difficult to refute was the suggestion, included in nearly all the press reports, that John's despair at the loss of his ship was so great that he had not tried to save his life when she sank. This idea was to give much agony to the Wordsworth family, and was not susceptible of proof either way, though it was much discussed. Most damaging of all was the persistent rumour that John was drunk in the last hours of the ship. It was denied from the first; *The Times* described him as 'a man of a cool and temperate disposition' and his employers, the East India Company, testified to the 'cool and even temperature of his blood' which made him most unlikely to have become drunk at such a moment. But the rumour continued to cast a shadow on his reputation. A year later Mrs Clarkson, friend of the Wordsworths and the Lambs, told Mary Lamb that she had heard a report that John was drunk when the ship sank. Mary Lamb replied with much indignation; the rumour came from an underwriter – insurers always tried to blame the captain when a ship sank, Charles had told her – 'but he had heard no whisper of such a rumour either at India House or elsewhere'. The gossip must have originated, she thought, with the story of Cornet Burgoyne giving John two glasses of cordial just at the last; no doubt this story 'was told from one to another, till at last the two glasses became a bottle and then the underwriters said he was drunk'. Burgoyne himself had spoken very handsomely about John's conduct in these last moments, and never suggested, or even heard it suggested, that John was then 'in liquor'. She added emphatically, 'We do not even think it possible for any quantity of liquor to make a man drunk in the agony of feeling he must have been in at that time.' Such a suggestion would give the utmost pain to the Wordsworths, and she hoped it would never reach their ears.

But it did reach the Wordsworth circle; John Rickman, Secretary to the Speaker of the House of Commons, told Southey that he heard there had been 'misconduct' over the sinking of the ship, a rumour which Southey strongly denied; the only misconduct had been that of the pilot in running her aground. The Southey and Coleridge families at Greta Hall thus knew of this story, and many years later Coleridge's daughter Sara mentioned that she had heard it said that 'Captain Wordsworth was perfectly stupefied when the danger came upon him and incapable of exertion', though she did add that the rumour was probably false. De Quincey, too, had heard the rumour during his connection with the Wordsworth circle, and in his essay on William in his *Reminiscences of the English Lake Poets* he still, as late as 1839, felt it necessary to deny the calumny that John was 'in a state of intoxication at the time

of the calamity', a slander quite incredible to anyone
who knew John's 'most temperate and even philo-
sophic habits of life'.

Apart from these main errors in published
accounts of the disaster, journalistic gloss added much
exaggeration even to the true facts they recorded.
The Times edified its readers by suggesting that the
Abergavenny's officers encouraged the men at the
pumps by 'a cheerful song and the smile of encourage-
ment' (which certainly sounds more decorous, if less
probable, than the allowance of grog to the pumpers
which was mentioned in another report), and by
having those left on board 'imploring the mercy of
their Creator' in despairing cries as the ship went
down. An article in the *Gentleman's Magazine*, not
content with praising Gilpin's courage as he rescued
and cheered his shipmates in the riggings, called on
its readers to revere 'the name of GILPIN, in whose
veins flows the milk of human kindness, not as a
tardy stream, but as a torrent'. A version of this
article which appeared in a Maltese journal, *Il
Cartaginese*, made still more of a meal of the catastrophe. Tides rush impetuously, the waves roar,
seagulls scream, the passengers are 'tortured by cruel
anxiety, with staring eyes and dejected hearts', they
utter deep sighs and 'broken sobs and tearful cries';
the officers behave with fearless calm, specially
Baggot, 'this generous youth in whose veins human
sensibility ran like a flood' (Baggot seems here to have

borrowed Gilpin's blood-content). The survivors in the shrouds greet their rescuers with tears as well as cheers and even, with supreme improbability, are said to have 'kissed the ropes which saved them'.

The most misleading flight of journalistic fantasy was displayed in a pamphlet, published anonymously on 13 February, with the resounding title of *An Authentic Narrative of the Loss of the Abergavenny, East Indiaman, off Portland, on the Night of the 5th February 1805, to which is added a return of the Passengers, Officers, Ship's Company, Troops etc. with the Age, Description and Birthplace of every Officer and Seaman, showing at one view the fate of each individual. Corrected from the Official Returns at the East India House.* This anonymous pamphlet had a quotation on its title page from Falconer's *Shipwreck*:

> Ha! Total night and horror here preside!
> My stunn'd ear tingles to the whizzing tide!
> It is the funeral knell; and gliding near,
> Methinks the phantoms of the dead appear.

These sensational lines set the tone for what was to follow. It was mainly a summary of information already printed in the newspapers, with rumours and anecdotes gleaned by the crowds outside East India House from the survivors as they arrived to report. But it included so much misinformation and exaggeration that it prompted East India House to commission one of its own staff, probably William

Dalmeida, to write another *Authentic Narrative* pamphlet which was published six days later, avowedly to correct the 'gross inaccuracies in a late publication'. Dalmeida's pamphlet had an almost identical title with the first *Authentic Narrative*, only adding John Wordsworth's name and the fact that it was 'Drawn from Official Documents and Commentaries from Various Respectable Survivors, By a Gentleman in the East India House'. It too had four lines of poetry on its title-page, from Clarence's dream in Shakespeare's *Richard III*.

> Lord! Lord! methought what pain it was to drown!
> What dreadful noise of waters in mine ears!
> What sights of ugly death within mine eyes!
> I thought I saw a thousand fearful wrecks.

Dalmeida corrected the errors about John having a wife and children, having been depressed before the ship sailed, having remained speechless and motionless after saying 'God's will be done'. He included in full Gilpin's memorandum which gave the most professional and reliable account of the wreck and what led up to it, and also some reports by Cornet Burgoyne, Cadet Baillie and other eyewitnesses. This pamphlet is rather pompous in tone, and shows a certain caution and defensiveness lest any blame for the wreck might attach to the East India Company. The previous *Authentic Narrative*, having got in first, and being written in a more readable style, proved to be the more influential source of legend about the shipwreck, particularly about the much-quoted dialogue between Baggot and John Wordsworth. 'We have done all we can, Sir – she will sink in a moment'; 'It cannot be helped. God's will be done.' This plain monosyllabic exchange was not nearly exciting enough for the anonymous author of the first *Authentic Narrative*, and the later reports based on it. In them Baggot was described as running up 'breathless' to deliver his message that 'all exertions were now in vain', and John as having 'steadfastly looked him in the face, and, at last, with every appearance of a heart-broken man, faintly answered', thereafter remaining speechless and motionless till the ship sank.

When it is remembered that this took place on a dark winter's night on the deck of a tossing ship about to sink amid a roar of wind and waves, the likelihood that the bystanders would have heard a faint voice or noticed a facial expression is not very great. They heard John's strong, not faint, voice speaking of God's will, and they heard his later talk and orders, but that did not make nearly such a good story.

The two *Authentic Narratives* were the first separate pamphlets to appear, but others were to follow. The most important was Cornet Burgoyne's. Next to Gilpin, Burgoyne gave the most detailed account by a survivor of the events of the *Abergavenny*'s last days and hours. He had reported to East India House on 7 February, and then went to the Prince of Wales Coffee House in Conduit Street, where both Charles and Mary Lamb tried to interview him, but by then he had left for Ireland. Later he published his own account of the disaster in a sixpenny pamphlet emphatically titled *A Correct Narrative of the Loss of the Earl of Abergavenny East Indiaman, Which Foundered in Weymouth Roads, on Tuesday Night February the 5th 1805*. In this pamphlet Burgoyne, though he seems to have been level-headed and helpful during the sinking, gives an impression of conceit and knowing best, bent on correcting everyone else, as the title of his pamphlet indicates. He opens in a tone of superiority: 'As two or three pamphlets of the loss of the Abergavenny have been published, which I know to be erroneous, and having been myself one of those who were so providentially saved by gaining the mizzen top, I flatter myself that the public will credit my Narrative before those that have been already circulated.' The account which follows is detailed and cogent, and on many points confirms Gilpin's story and other survivors' accounts. There are, however, some important differences. Gilpin had said that the boats could not have been hoisted without laying the main topsail aback, which would have slowed down the ship's progress towards grounding on Weymouth Sands. Burgoyne denied this, maintaining that after the sails were lowered,

> the main yard might have been squared, and the boats got out. I myself having been at sea for several years, must know, and will appeal to any person that is a seaman, that if you want to pay a ship's head round off, you must square your after yards, therefore instead of impeding her, it was assisting her; besides, there was a cutter hanging to the starboard quarter which was never attempted to be lowered down, that boat went down with the ship.

It is difficult to see how Burgoyne, who was still only a cornet (second-lieutenant, the lowest commissioned rank in the cavalry) could already have spent several years at sea, whereas Gilpin had spent all his working life at sea, labouring his way up from midshipman to fourth mate, and may be supposed more experienced in seamanship than a junior Army officer. Burgoyne was perhaps jealous of Gilpin, who had been widely praised in the newspapers for his courage and leadership. Burgoyne was one of those who maintained that it was the sixth mate, Mortimer, not Gilpin, who went back to rescue Sergeant Hart from the riggings. It will be remembered that Burgoyne had only been on board for eight days, and may not in that time have got to know which was which of the ship's officers.

Burgoyne ridiculed the rumour that the cries of drowning men were heard as far away as Lulworth, more than seven miles away to the north-east; even when he was directly above the drowning men, perched on the topmast, he could scarcely hear their cries because of the roar of wind and waves. He also denied the story about Baggot being drowned while trying to rescue Mrs Blair. He maintained that Baggot was on the poop when the ship was sinking, and went down the ladder to get into the longboat which was in the booms, but before he could do so, he was over-powered by the advancing wave and went down with the ship. The two accounts, however, are not incom-patible. Baggot, like others who did survive, could have been swept into the sea and kept himself afloat by clinging to a spar till he was all but saved by the sloop which rescued the men from the riggings, but died trying to pull Mrs Blair to safety. Burgoyne's desire to score off others whom he 'knew to be erroneous' makes his vivid and observant account not totally reliable.

Confusingly, yet another *Correct Statement of the Loss of the Abergavenny* was published in London by Thomas Tegg, but it is of no value, simply a compo-site of the two *Authentic Narratives* and Burgoyne's *Correct Narrative*, incorporating all the exaggerations about faint voices and heartbroken facial expressions. It also included the fanciful, but rather striking engraving of the rescue from the shrouds *[Plate 8]* and a remarkably soppy set of verses by Laura Sophia Temple (which sounds like a pseudonym), said to have been published on the occasion of the wreck, and full of personifications of Valour, Fancy, Fortune, Beauty, Time, Nature and Thought intruding themselves into the action; of gallant but hapless youths with manly brows, widowed hearts, and orphans' uplifted tearful eyes.

The catastrophe inspired another even more high-flown poem. John Barlow, a Dorset schoolmaster, opened his *The Loss of the Abergavenny, East India-man: a Poem with Notes* with a resounding tribute to commerce which might have been produced by the Company to advertise their activities and act as a caption to the allegory in the pediment of East India House.

> A gen'rous interchange of distant wealth
> At once does honour to a nation's name,
> And forms a band of friendship and of faith
> Between remotest regions of the globe.
> Hail honourable commerce: gentle gales
> And heav'n propitious crown thy safe return:
> But heav'n's immutable yet just decree
> May guide the pirate thro' the tempest's rage,
> And give the honest merchant up a prey.
> Such was thy fate, O WORDSWORTH.

The rest of the poem is a farrago of heroic deeds, manly crew, purple-blooming youth, sorrowing parents, horrors of the deep, the ruthless element, the

wan orb of night, consternation, dreadful visitations
and despairing cries –

Great source of mercy, what a shriek was there!

To mock such attitudinizing is fair game, but it is
not easy for journalists – or biographers – to get
catastrophe-reporting right, as many of them have
recently found in many corners of the world from
floods in Mozambique to massacres in Kosovo. Quote
what victims and survivors actually said, and it will
sound flat and inadequate; famous last words do not
prove as impressive as one would wish. A year after
the loss of the *Abergavenny*, the younger Pitt was lying
on his deathbed, and one of the watchers beside him
remembered his tragic death cry as 'Oh, my country!
how I leave my country!'; but a nurse who was in
attendance thought that the last thing he said was to
ask for some barley water, and a doorkeeper at the
House of Commons related that the expiring states-
man's last utterance was 'I think I could eat one
of Bellamy's pork pies.' If sufferers will not strike
an appropriate attitude naturally, the temptation to
arrange them into one is great. But if yielded to, it
can produce compassion fatigue, even ridicule. If the
story is told with too much heightening and side-
taking, readers will feel they are being got at. If they
are given surmises as to what the victims must have
felt, readers will ask, 'What proof have you of that?'
If authenticated facts are simply presented without

comment, readers will be bored; they want drama and pathos, not barley water and pork pies. Eyewitnesses contradict each other, second-hand rumours are sworn to as verified fact. Choice of which events to report, however conscientiously made with a view to being fair to all concerned, in itself imposes a bias. No calamity is ever described with perfect truth; the ripples of the flood, the echoes of the massacre, die away in the distance beyond recall.

Chapter Ten

THE NEWS OF THE shipwreck did not reach the Lake District until 11 February. That morning Sara Hutchinson, who was staying with Thomas and Elizabeth Cookson at Kendal, discovered it, probably from a newspaper. Southey, who also heard it that morning in Keswick, said that 'the news came flying up to us from all quarters'. Sara started off at once to be with the Wordsworths, collecting their letters from the post office as she passed through Ambleside.

She arrived at Dove Cottage at two o'clock that afternoon, and found only Dorothy at home – William and Mary were out walking. The shock of the news contained in the letter from Richard Wordsworth which Sara had brought from Ambleside therefore fell full on Dorothy without warning; William had no chance to break it gently to her. Richard's letter was a stiff communication of a few lines, giving the bare facts of John's death and the loss of the ship, in conventional words such as 'painful concern' and 'melancholy event', and recommending William to do what – as it turned out – he had no chance to do, to 'impart this to Dorothy in the best manner you can'. William and Mary returned from their walk to be confronted with the dreadful news and with Dorothy in a state of miserable affliction. William spent the next few hours in trying to console Dorothy and Mary, who was almost equally wretched; William knew that his wife loved John as a brother, almost as much as his own brother and sister did, and for many hours of weeping neither Dorothy nor Mary could bear to hear a word about the wreck. William himself was much in need of consolation at the loss of his 'ever dear Brother'. At nine o'clock that night he brought himself to reply to Richard's letter, asking for full information about the catastrophe, and dwelling more on Dorothy's state of mind than his own; but he paid the first of very many tributes to John's memory which he was to include in long mournful letters in the weeks to come. 'John was very dear to me and my heart will never forget him. God rest his soul!'

He also wrote that night to his friend Sir George Beaumont, in reply to a letter which had arrived simultaneously with the one from Richard breaking the news. To the sympathetic Beaumont, William revealed more of his feelings than he had to his brother Richard. 'I can say nothing higher of my ever dear Brother than that he was worthy of his sister who is now weeping beside me, and of the friendship of Coleridge; meek, affectionate, silently enthusiastic, loving all quiet things, and a Poet in everything but words.' Already a Grasmere image of John is beginning to emerge which perhaps would not have been perfectly recognizable to his ship's company.

Next day all the inmates of the house of mourning spent much of the time in tears, and William had no shame about admitting this. 'We weep much today, and that relieves us. As to fortitude, I hope I shall show that, and that all of us will show it, in a proper time, in keeping down many a silent pang hereafter. But grief will ... and must have its course; there is no wisdom in attempting to check it under the circumstances which we are all of us in here.' The stiff upper lip for men had not then come into fashion. William's idea that giving way to one's feelings at first might help one to fortitude later seems psychologically sound. 'At present I weep with them and attempt little more,' he owned.

Sara Hutchinson, who had hastened to Dove Cottage 'to be of use in the house and to comfort us,' as William gratefully put it, was a helpful presence and support; he blessed her for the good she had done to them all. Southey was another friend who rallied to the shattered family's support. He had heard the news before they did, and it had shocked him grievously, all the more because he dreaded that he might have to be the first to break the news to William, who was expected to call shortly at Greta Hall. Southey tried, as was his usual custom in times of grief, to master it by mental exertion, a difficult but not impossible feat, he found; but at night his dreams were dreadful. He wrote at once to William, at a loss as to what he could say in face of such a thunderstroke, but offering to come over to Dove Cottage, or to have William at Greta Hall, as soon as William felt that a friend's company would be any help. William replied that he would be for ever thankful if Southey would come next day to Dove Cottage, so Southey arrived there on the 13th and stayed until the 15th. In those days he won Dorothy's grateful affection. Till then, she had admired and liked him to some extent, but thought him lacking in dignity and enthusiasm. But when he came to them after John's death 'he was so tender and kind that I loved him all at once – he wept with us in our sorrow, and for that cause I think I must always love him'. William too was grateful to Southey, who was a great comfort to them all while he stayed at Dove Cottage, promised to return again soon, and endeared himself for ever to the grieving family by his sympathy.

The grief that each member of the household felt was doubled by the compassion each felt for the sorrow the others were enduring. Dorothy was the prime anxiety of her brother and sister-in-law, and though William felt he had been of some use to her during the dreadful twelve hours after the news first arrived, he and Mary were deeply concerned that her health would break down. She was very ill on that

first day, and though in the following days her actual
bodily health was better, she still suffered from 'sickness of the stomach', and he knew that her sorrow
would be long-lasting and poignant. As always,
Dorothy's first concern was for William's feelings,
but she also recognized Mary's own sincere mourning for John, and was anxious about the effect of his
death on the other brothers Richard and Christopher,
though she had not the strength to write her sympathy
for a fortnight to come. William discouraged her from
trying to write any letters, as he thought it would
'cleave her heart in pieces'; all the accounts of these
first days of sorrow come from William's letters. Mary
was a great comfort and consolation to Dorothy, but
she too thought first of all of William's feelings, and
admitted the justice of his strangely egoistical claim
that the loss was worst of all for him. 'Our beloved
William!' she wrote, '. . . could you but know how he
has exerted himself to comfort us and, after all, as
he tells us, his is the greatest loss – because he says it
is only our pleasures and our joys that are broken in
upon – but loss of John is deeply connected with his
business. This is true – but is not his sorrow ours.'
William's 'business' was of course writing poetry, and
John's contribution to this which William had now
lost was John's admiration and sympathetic criticism
of his brother's poetry – 'I never wrote a line without
a thought of its giving him pleasure', William
declared – and John's promise to provide the money

in which the women could not bear to hear details of the wreck, they began to want to know exactly what had happened. William had said, even on that first evening, that to hear as minutely as possible how it had happened would be a comfort in their loneliness, and Dorothy, as soon as she felt capable of writing to Richard, asked him to enquire about John's last moments, and whether anything of his had been recovered from the wreck. She got little satisfaction from Richard, who simply said it was impossible for him to enter into particulars about the catastrophe, he could only say that John had done everything possible in his desperate situation. This was not much comfort to William and Dorothy, and they appealed for more information to a more sympathetic and authoritative source, someone who actually worked in East India House – their and John's old friend Charles Lamb.

In reply to William's letter of enquiry, Lamb wrote on 18 February with perceptive sympathy about John's death. Lamb was seriously unwell at the time, and wrote with difficulty, his sister Mary sitting crying by his side as he wrote. Both of them felt deeply how much the Wordsworths must be suffering, and warmly recalled their own memories of John, of his fine appearance and voice, his pride in his profession, and how happy they had all been together when he visited the Lambs in London between voyages; 'he was a cheerful soul!' Lamb told William what news he had been able to collect so far about the wreck. He had seen the newspaper reports and heard various second-hand accounts, but so far had only managed one face-to-face interview with a survivor, the second mate W. G. E. Stewart, who had not been able to tell him anything about John's last moments, as he had been in another part of the ship when she went down. Lamb would write again when he had seen more of the survivors, especially the fourth mate Gilpin.

At this stage Lamb had not realized how strongly William felt about whether John had been active to the last, and tried to save his life when the ship sank. So Lamb passed on the current general opinion that, though John had done all that duty required, and was under no reproach, 'he seemed like one overwhelmed with the situation, and careless of his own safety'. But next day he wrote again after an interview with Gilpin, passing on Gilpin's assurance that John had been heard calmly giving orders just before the ship went down, and did not neglect his own safety through distraction of mind. William seized eagerly on this evidence, and both he and Dorothy emphasized in their letters how false, and how cruel to the families of others who were drowned, was the rumour that John had been too much overcome to take the necessary action to save his ship and himself.

Lamb did all he could to censor information about the wreck that might reach the Wordsworths. He told them of the existence of the two *Authentic Narrative*

the midshipman Benjamin Yates, who gave his opinion that John had not wanted to survive the loss of his ship, was brushed aside by Lamb as a 'young seaman' who could not have known John's 'inner man'. Perhaps, Lamb suggested, John had suffered some blow when the ship went down, and this disabled him from saving himself by swimming.

Lamb was determined to do all he could to console the Wordsworths by seeking out the fullest details; he begged William not to spare him in asking for his good offices in any way he could help. 'Adopt me as one of your family in this affliction; and use me without ceremony as such,' he wrote. So he not only sought out and interviewed Gilpin and Second Mate Stewart, but sent further questions to Gilpin, who had already been appointed to another East Indiaman, the *Comet*, and was at Gravesend. He also got a colleague in East India House, who was a cousin of Benjamin Yates, to send a questionnaire for Yates to answer. He tried, but failed, to get in touch with Webber, who had been standing close to John when the ship sank. He even got hold of someone in one of the other East Indiamen of the convoy which were anchored in Portland Roads while the *Abergavenny* was sinking, who was able to explain why her signal guns, which some reports suggested had never been fired, were not heard by the other convoy ships. He wrote to Cornet Burgoyne to ask him to send William his version of the events of the shipwreck. No answer came from Burgoyne, who had been staying in a London coffee house since he came up to London after the shipwreck, so Mary Lamb called there twice, only to find that Burgoyne had left for Ireland. Intrepidly she engaged in a long conversation with the innkeeper of the coffee house, who may have found it queer to be lengthily cross-examined about a shipwreck by a square snuff-sprinkled old maid, even if he was unaware that she periodically went out of her mind. Burgoyne had discussed the wreck with the innkeeper, and Mary Lamb was able to bring back a report that Burgoyne had spoken very handsomely of John, and imputed no blame to him for what had happened. In his later pamphlet Burgoyne, who was close to John when the ship went down, testified that Gilpin had tried to save John, but he was too exhausted to respond and 'sank to rise no more'.

William and Dorothy themselves had always been convinced that John must have shown calm, authority and courage in his last hours, but it was a comfort to receive evidence that public opinion shared their conviction.

> The newspapers have given contrary and unintelligible accounts of the dismal event – this was very harassing to us [wrote Dorothy a month after they first heard the news]. We knew that our Brother would do his duty, of this we were confident – that

he would not lose his presence of mind, or blunder. or forget, but we wanted to have all cleared up, to know *how* it was. This as far as concerned ourselves – and then for the sake of the relatives of those poor three hundred who went down with him we were greatly distressed. It cut us to the heart to think that their sorrow should be aggravated by a thought that his errors or weakness, or any other misconduct should have occasioned or increased the calamity.

But now the story of the wreck was known to everybody, and as the first weeks of mourning misery passed, both William and Dorothy began to be able to write letters to their friends filled with ever-increasing praise and admiration for their lost brother.

Chapter Eleven

AT DAWN ON THE MORNING of 6 February, after the survivors of the *Abergavenny* had been brought ashore, the watchers on Weymouth Beach could still see the ship's topmasts and shrouds standing up from the surface a mile and a half out to sea, though during the night she had settled deeper into the seabed, on an even keel, at ten fathoms. The mayor and aldermen, and other inhabitants of Weymouth, rallied to the aid of the victims, looking after the survivors who were dying or recovering from hypothermia, collecting the bodies washed ashore and arranging for their funerals. Most of the bodies were washed up on the beach below Wyke Regis, though some were carried as far as Melcombe Regis and Radipole. The bodies of Cadet Forbes and Sergeant Hart, who died on shore after being rescued, were buried on 8 February with military honours, but John Wordsworth's corpse was not to be recovered for another six weeks, Mrs Blair's not until 23 April, and Baggot's, 'much disfigured', not till 19 July.

At Dove Cottage they were waiting to hear whether John's body, or any of his possessions – his writing-desk or his telescope – had been recovered from the wreck, which they could have and treasure in his memory. William, who had heard that some bodies from the wreck had already been washed ashore, tried to get Richard to write to the clergyman, or whoever would be the appropriate person, at Weymouth, to arrange for John to be properly buried in a separate grave if his body was found; this was usually done for officers – other bodies would be thrown into a common grave at the expense of the parish.

John's body was found on 20 March by a dragging operation quite near the sunken ship. It was identified by the purser Stewart, who had accepted the job of agent for the underwriters in Weymouth, and was fixed there for the time, occupied in the gruesome task of identifying the bodies as they were washed ashore. He wrote to Captain John Wordsworth senior on 22 March:

'I have the melancholy pleasure of acquainting you that the body of your late unfortunate Cousin has been recovered by dragging, and that fortunately being on the spot I could fully identify his person . . . Excuse my writing more fully at present, or in detail, of the unfortunate Bodies daily now brought on shore, they are too shocking to dwell upon, and almost too replete with horror for a

parent's feelings ... I am now going to view more
bodies in hopes to ascertain that of my lost Child
or poor Baggot'.

He enclosed a sketch map of the locale of the wreck
[Plate 9] and added that, as the Wordsworth family
had requested, he would offer a reward for John's
sword if it was recovered from the wreck.

Stewart had to remain in Weymouth identifying bodies, including Mrs Blair's and Baggot's, all
through the spring and summer. He was described as
having been 'constantly and kindly attentive to the
last offices of Christian friendship'. There is no record
of whether he ever had to identify the body of his
own son, his 'lost Child'.

John's body was taken for burial to All Saints, the
parish church of Wyke Regis *[Plate 10]*. The suburbs
of Weymouth have now spread to encircle this
fifteenth-century church with its square bell tower,
for centuries a landmark for sailors in Lyme Bay to
the west; but in 1805 it stood in open country among
downs, with only a few nearby cottages. There had
been an earlier church there since the twelfth century,
and it was regarded as the mother church of Weymouth. Its graveyard was used for mass burials of
those lost at sea.

John's funeral cortège was attended by a former
mayor of Weymouth, the officer commanding the local
Sea Fencibles, Stewart representing the East India

Company, an escort of twelve marines, and many local inhabitants. The funeral arrangements were said to have been made by Mrs Bristow, a relation of Christopher Wordsworth's wife (or, according to another version, by 'an aunt of Mr C. Wordsworth'). Church records suggest that John's body was buried in a separate grave on the south side of the church; another tradition places his grave on the north side; but in 1932 a descendant of a Portland family remembered hearing from her grandmother (born in 1782) that all the bodies recovered from the wreck, as many as eighty, were buried in a huge pit dug just inside the churchyard wall on the south side of the church, and that a large stone, actually one of the church's altar slabs, was placed over the mass burial, but was later returned to the interior of the church. There is now no gravestone or slab at Wyke Regis to show where John and his shipmates were buried. In 1904 a memorial stone of Westmorland slate was erected in Grasmere churchyard, describing John as 'silent poet' and 'cherished visitant and lover of this valley'.

There was no possibility that William and Dorothy could have attended the funeral; they did not even hear that the body had been found till a week after it was buried. It was perhaps as well; if he really was buried with eighty others in a mass grave, it would have been additionally distressing to find that Richard had apparently taken no action on William's suggestion about arranging a fitting separate burial for him.

But if the tradition about the separate grave is the right one, perhaps Christopher Wordsworth's connection did carry out the family's wishes.

Dorothy found it a great comfort to know that John's body had been buried – 'his grave is a resting-place for our thoughts' – and she looked forward to their being able to visit the grave some day. William's resting-place for his thoughts of John's grave was in imagining that daisies – which John had once described, in a poetic burst rare in his letters, as 'like little white stars upon the dark green fields' of the Isle of Wight – would grow on his grave.

~~~

ON 24 APRIL there was a strong south-easterly gale in Weymouth Bay, and part of the submerged deck of the wreck was broken up by the violent motion of the waves. Articles from the wreck as well as about thirty bodies, were washed up on the shore, and many Weymouth inhabitants spent the night walking on the beach with lights, to pick up the articles thrown up on the sands.

Salvage from the wreck had begun almost at once. A cutter was sent out to guard it and to strip the riggings from the masts, and a little later the masts and yards were brought into Weymouth. In March, at the request of the East India Company, the Admiralty ordered the Commander-in-Chief at Portsmouth to station a cutter or brig permanently beside the wreck to protect the cargo and stores. Rumours of the rich cargo in the ship had been widespread, and applications from salvage firms for the job of recovering the cargo poured into East India House. Minor objects from the wreck were recovered duing the summer of 1805, and in September an expert salvager, John Braithwaite, began the task, using explosives to get through the thick timbers of the ship's hull to reach the cargo, enabling him in April 1806 to start bringing up sixty-two chests of silver dollars, each chest containing the equivalent of £1,200.

Braithwaite's journal of the salvage process lists an extraordinary collection of artefacts brought up from the wreck, giving a vivid impression of the passengers' personal possessions as well as the cargo. The list included lead, iron 'knees', bales of cloth, Irish linen, a box of silk stockings, a box of gloves, silk handkerchiefs, pieces of silk, black muslin, ribbon, a hamper of ale, a large chest of books, a quantity of 'Great Coats for hot countries', ebony and glass inkstands, a small case of liqueurs, saddles, bridles and chaise harness, boots, millinery, knives, perfumery, three trunks, and cases of looking-glasses. The salvage went on through 1806, but by March 1807 'the cargo got so thin, not worth getting up'.

Intermittently for the next hundred and seventy years the wreck was explored by divers, blown apart by salvagers in search of copper fastening, possibly flattened by the Navy as a danger to shipping entering

Portland Harbour; and at some time during these years John Wordsworth's sword was found and returned to his family. It was not until 1979 that a systematic exploration of the wreck was begun by the Chelmsford Sub Aqua Club, and is still continuing. They have already brought up a fascinating collection of artefacts from the wreck: inkpots, toothbrushes, medical vials, coins, a gold chain and rings (were these the property of the three women passengers, Emilia Evans, Rebecca Jackson and Margaret Blair?), bottle stoppers, belt buckles and one brass label for a sea chest whose ownership can be definitely assigned to one man on board, as it bears the name of John Forbes, the cadet who died after being rescued from the sea. A recent recovery from the wreck is a pair of cufflinks initialled 'J.W.'; it seems possible that these were John Wordsworth's own [Plates 11, 12, 13, 14, 15].

Cornet Burgoyne, on the other hand, was doubly lucky; not only did he survive the wreck, but he got his baggage back. At the end of February a Dorset parson, the Revd Mr Coates, rector of the parish of Osmington, wrote to East India House to say that he had preserved from plunder a trunk which had floated ashore from the wreck and been found on the beach by some of his parishioners who brought it to him. Its contents showed that it belonged to Burgoyne, who went down to Osmington at once to collect it. It contained his will and other papers, and a large sum of money – £1,500 according to some of the press reports – in cash, so both the Osmington parishioners and their rector deserve some credit for not 'plundering' it.

Other survivors were not so fortunate; although several more trunks were washed ashore, they were all empty, and claims for compensation for property lost in the wreck began to reach East India House. The Court of Directors had decided on 13 February that the enquiry into the loss of the *Abergavenny* should be referred to its Committee of Shipping, which would interrogate the surviving officers on the 19th and 20th. While the Court was awaiting the Committee's report, it turned its attention to the compensation claims. First it decided that 'in consideration of the severe losses in Baggage and Passage Money' experienced by the surviving Company cadets, Gramshaw, Baillie, Johnstone, Thwaites and Taylor, they should be awarded £100 each when they made their second try to sail to India. Baillie, however, asked to defer his departure for India till the following season; his health had suffered, his father had just died – plainly he could not face the sea again just yet. The Court of Directors, just rather than generous, allowed him to stay in England for another year and not to lose his rank in the cadets' order of seniority, but he was not to have the £100 compensation awarded to him till he did sail to India next year.

The next claims to be considered were those of the surviving ship's officers and petty officers, who had written 'entreating the Court's favourable consideration of their distressed case' and asking for a gratuity to pay for their replacement outfits and other losses. The Court awarded them gratuities in strict order of seniority: £100 each for Second Mate Stewart and Third Mate Joseph Wordsworth, £75 for Fourth Mate Gilpin, £50 each for Purser Stewart and Surgeon Davie, £40 each for the fifth and sixth mates, £20 each for Gunner Abbott, Carpenter Atwater and Ship's Steward Akers, £10 each for the five midshipmen and £5 for Caulker Mackay. But they added a special decision that Fourth Mate Gilpin, 'in consequence of his very meritorious Conduct after the ship had sunk be presented with an additional gratuity of £25 to purchase a piece of plate'.

This decision marked, without having to say so openly, that Gilpin deserved at least as much compensation as Joseph Wordsworth, who had been taken safely to shore by boat long before the ship sank, and Second Mate Stewart, whose part in the events was not illuminated by much glory. It is not known where he was when the ship went down, except that he was nowhere near John and the other officers on the poop. None of the press reports, so lavish in their praise of the conduct of John, Baggot and Gilpin during the ship's last hours, mentioned Stewart at all. He did not come to London till 12 February, when he wrote to East India House to say that he was 'awaiting the Council's pleasure'. Lamb interviewed him on 18 February, but could get no satisfactory account from him as to what had happened. Perhaps the pointed special award to Gilpin for meritorious conduct aroused his envy; a month later he petitioned the Court of Directors that 'in view of his past services and losses' he should be appointed commander of the new ship which was to be built to replace the *Abergavenny*. The Directors' Court Book recorded this petition without comment. Perhaps it was made clear to him that he was opening his mouth too wide, perhaps he himself awoke to a more realistic view of his position; a month later he withdrew his application to be commander of the new ship – he had accepted a berth in the *Preston* at his old rank of Second Mate.

The last compensation claims to be considered by the Court of Directors were those of the widows and children of drowned men of the ship's company. In mid-March the widows of carpenters, cooks, sailmakers, gunners and armourers petitioned for relief, which was granted on a somewhat meagre scale, including extra annual grants for children until they were old enough to earn their own livings. Sarah Goham, wife of the boatswain, got the highest amount – £9 12s od a year, and £1 18s 5d a year for her two children.

The Committee of Shipping completed its enquiry

into the wreck and reported to the full Court of Directors, who on 26 February 'resolved unanimously that the Commander, Officers and Ship's Company of the Earl of Abergavenny be fully acquitted of all Imputation of Neglect or Misconduct in respect to the loss of that Ship'. John's reputation, like his sword, came back whole from the sea to sustain his family's pride in him.

A FORTNIGHT after the news of John's death reached Dove Cottage, William was able to write: 'We are all somewhat easier in mind, much *easier* I might say; but our *grief* is of a kind which time only can alleviate. We know what we have lost, and what we have to endure; our anguish is allayed, but pain and sadness have taken place of it; with fits of sorrow which we endeavour to suppress but cannot.' His and Dorothy's letters in the next few weeks relate that they were becoming more composed in mind, that at intervals at least their thoughts were calmer and more settled, that they had even had some cheerful and happy moments.

Some of their causes for concern had now ceased. John's body had been found and buried. His courage and leadership had been fully vindicated to the public by the Court of Enquiry at East India House. Word had come from Richard Wordsworth that William's and Dorothy's investment in the ship was fully covered by insurance. Sir George Beaumont had written with anxious friendship to ask whether the Wordsworths would suffer financially as well as emotionally from the loss of the ship. William replied with a detailed account of the family's financial resources, in reply to which Sir George sent him a present of money. This evoked from William a lengthy meditation on the ethics of men of letters receiving money gifts from strangers or from friends, ending in acceptance of Sir George's present which, though not needed for the Wordsworths' immediate necessities, would be 'of serious benefit to the minds and healths of us all'; it would enable them all to go on a much-needed holiday in the summer, William could buy some books he wanted and he could concentrate on writing poetry instead of trying to earn money by literary drudgery, for which he was at present quite unfit.

The lifting of these burdens helped the family to return to their normal routine. Dorothy got up at seven and dressed and fed the children; she and Mary shared their care, each looking after them for half the day, and this was a helpful distraction, though Dorothy found the baby's quietness more soothing than Johnny's irrepressible boisterousness. He was beginning to talk, Mary told Mrs Clarkson, and added, 'These dear Darlings beguile me of many a melancholy moment – yet how many melancholy thoughts do they bring to us all – O! how dearly their Uncle would have loved them! and what an example he would have been to them. This may still be. It shall be one of their first lessons to honour and reverence his memory. O Mrs Clarkson he shall live amongst us for ever.' This was Mary's farewell to the man who had loved her devotedly; she never mentioned him again in any surviving letter.

Other aspects of the Wordsworths' return to their usual occupations showed this mixture of consoling normality and constant reminder of their loss. Whenever they went into their garden and orchard they saw trees that John had planted; now that they had resumed their daily walks, they were constantly revisiting places and prospects that they had seen with him. Dorothy, whose health was less affected than her family had feared, though she looked thin and ill and found it difficult to sleep, had started writing letters again, and this occupation too was both upsetting and soothing. It made her weep to write to her friends about John, but like William she thought that tears were cathartic, and that it was better not to try to restrain them. It even did her good when friends like Southey and Mrs Lloyd who came to Dove Cottage wept with her.

The Wordsworths' emotions were strong, but so were their minds; they could think how to manage and learn from their grief, to see what part it might play in their future lives and plans. Dorothy analysed which of her consolations came to her in gusts of feeling, and which in the quiet growth of her mind.

She looked forward to the time when she would become more worthy of John's example, better and even happier because he had lived. 'The time will come when the light of the setting Sun upon these mountain tops will be as heretofore a pure joy – not the same *gladness*, that can never be – but yet a joy even more tender.' William believed that eventually when his mind was calmer, he would find that John's example and memory would animate him in his poetic vocation even more than the joy he had felt in John's living presence had done. They were beginning to look ahead to new patterns of life. Perhaps they would all find refreshment in a summer tour that year; almost certainly they would move from Dove Cottage – it was now too small for them, and too much associated with sad memories.

Meanwhile, the best therapy for William would be a return to writing poetry. He had felt from the first a strong impulse to write a poem about John's virtues. He began it, and such a torrent of poetry tore through his mind that he was overpowered and had to stop, and he afterwards found that all but a few lines of it had vanished from his memory, as he had been unable, as was his usual practice, to dictate what he had composed to Mary or Dorothy; the subject would have distressed them too much, he thought. But Dorothy felt it was an imperative duty of hers and Mary's to raise William's spirits so that he could return to writing poetry. The first work she was able to do after John's death was to transcribe some of his previous poems, and by mid-April she was able to tell Lady Beaumont that he had started writing again – not yet a poem dedicated entirely to John, but he had resumed his work on the growth of his own mind which would eventually become *The Prelude*.

If William could not yet write a poem on John's virtues, he suffered no writer's block in expatiating on them in his letters. All through February, March and April he wrote long letters to Beaumont, to Thomas Clarkson, to James Losh and to Sir Walter Scott, celebrating over and over again John's good qualities. John had been meek, gentle, modest, tender-hearted, affectionate, enthusiastic, but also rational, sedate, prudent and self-controlled. He was brave, resolute, noble in countenance and bearing, pure-minded, happy-tempered, beloved and honoured by everyone. He was well-read, full of taste, genius, intellectual merit, a silent poet. He was a totally congenial companion and sharer of his siblings' tastes and feelings as well as their brother in blood, and he was unselfishly dedicated to helping them.

It was a towering tumulus of memorial tributes. One modern commentator has actually taken the trouble to list the number of times William repeated each of the eulogies. William himself admitted that John would have been shocked by the manner in which William had praised him, but insisted that it was far below the truth. John did not know how much

William had loved and honoured him, how often he had thought of him.

The sting of that thought – that in John's lifetime it had not been fully apparent what his family thought of him – perhaps pricked William into his outburst of posthumous praise. The *de mortuis nil nisi bonum* principle was not peculiar to the Wordsworths, but its operation is not often shown in such fullness as it was by them. Did they remember that John had once been thought a dunce, the least clever of his brothers, abnormally shy, usually referred to as 'poor John'? Were they casting a retrospective glamour in their minds over the 'eight blessed months', as William now called them, in 1800 when they had all been so happy together at Dove Cottage? John now seemed to all of them – to William, to Dorothy, to Mary – to have been almost their leader in those blissful months; but Dorothy's journal, actually written at the time, does not highlight him. He fishes, bathes, walks, alone or with the others, he chats with Dorothy and Coleridge, but it is William, as always, who is in the centre of Dorothy's attention. She sits up to wait for the brothers' return from a visit to Yorkshire. 'After 11 o'clock I heard a foot go to the front of the house, turn round, and open the gate. It was William!' It was John, too, but he did not get a mention in the journal entry.

There is no doubt that both William and Dorothy did love their brother dearly, and felt deep, sincere and lasting grief over his death. That reality is not impugned by the possible presence of a tinge of that remorse which is so often felt by other mourners at not having sufficiently valued the lost beloved ones in their lifetime. It is possible that they now felt they had taken him too much for granted, not noticed and observed him enough, not shown him how highly they thought of him. Dorothy may have felt that she had been too exclusively focused on William; William may have realized that his self-absorption had prevented him from seeing that John was in love with Mary when she was still Mary Hutchinson. It could have been partly self-reproach that made them verge on canonization in their memories of him, turning 'John, poor dear fellow' almost into 'Saint John'.

Chapter Thirteen

JOHN WORDSWORTH'S death and the loss of his ship cast a cold shadow over the life and work of his friends, as well as his family.

Coming at a crucial moment in the life-work of Thomas Clarkson and William Wilberforce, it distracted their attention for a time from their great cause, the liberation of the slaves. Wilberforce had seen much of John in the previous autumn, when he had used his influence to secure for John his heart's desire of the most favourable route to China for his forthcoming voyage. Thomas Clarkson and his wife Catherine had become close friends of the Wordsworths when they lived in the Lake District. Mrs Clarkson was a sickly, witty, warm-hearted woman who became a lifelong friend and correspondent of Dorothy's. Her husband, a dedicated and high-minded but rather prosaic and tedious character, was preoccupied by his mission to bring about the abolition of the slave trade, an aim of which he and Wilberforce were the chief promoters.

In that month of February 1805, the House of Commons was deliberating on a bill to abolish the slave trade, which Wilberforce had again introduced to the House after previous defeats. The final vote on the second reading of the bill was to be on 28 February, and Wilberforce and Clarkson were both occupied in organizing support. At noon on 16 February, William Wordsworth wrote to Clarkson to tell him the dreadful news about John, but Clarkson had already heard it. A fortnight later he wrote a sympathetic but orotund letter to William.

> I do most truly condole with you with the most sincere of all mournings, the Mourning of the Heart. I mourn both for you and for Dorothy, and for Mrs Wordsworth, because I see no End or Measure of your Grief, and I mourn for my lost Friend, not only on account of the Loss to you, but of his Loss as a Man. I believe that, if he had returned, and settled in Life, he would have been useful in his Day, by the practical Duty of Benevolence, and by his Example to others. But so it has pleased Providence, and if we cannot call him back, we must reverence his Memory, by the Imitation of his Virtue.

Clarkson went on to describe the effect of John's death on Wilberforce as well as himself, and how it had disrupted their labours.

> On the day when I first heard of the mournful news I had left Wilberforce's house and was upon 'Change. I cannot tell you what my feelings were,

or the almost convulsed State between Hope and
Fear. It was reported that only 73 had been saved,
and that his Name was not among them. At one
time I thought of writing to you to apprise you
gently of the Event, but in two hours' time I heard
upon a certainty that 120 were saved though his
name again was not among them ... On my return
to Wilberforce's in the evening, he apprised me of
the Certainty of the Event and of the Certainty
of the Individual Loss, which he had heard from an
India Director at the House of Commons: and here
I cannot help observing that I saw the tear come
into his Eyes while he repeated it. He called to mind
your Brother's modest and unaffected manner; he
considered himself as the Patron of a young man
who was lost: and his Grief continued without inter-
mission for the three days I was with him,
mentioning the Circumstances and the Character of
your Brother, to all his friends. During all this time,
when I ought to have been employed every minute
in writing on the Abolition, I found my own labours
were suspended, for I had no power of attending to
what it was proper to write.

~~~

On Southey, the effect of the news – when he sat
back to consider it after first doing what he could for
William, by letter and by offering a visit if that would
help – was to speculate on the psychological effect of
disaster reports, especially accounts of shipwrecks, on
both writers and readers of such accounts, and how

it was likely to affect his own writing. In that winter of 1804–5 he had been, not unusually for him, working very hard. When he heard the news about John in mid-February his epic *Madoc* had just gone to the printers, he was revising *Joan of Arc*, contributing articles to the *Annual Review*, and making progress with his *History of Portugal*. It was this last work that might be affected by the loss of the *Abergavenny*, the news of which, he said, made his very flesh quiver; it came home to him all the more because of his fears for his brother Tom, a lieutenant in the Royal Navy, who was experiencing frequent near escapes from shipwreck, or capture by the French, in his ship on the West India station. Southey wrote to a friend, on the day he heard the news of John's death, that 'what renders any near loss of the kind so peculiarly distressing is, that the recollection is perpetually freshened when any like event occurs, by the mere mention of shipwreck, or the sound of the wind. Of all deaths it is the most dreadful, from the circumstances of terror which accompany it.' He foresaw that he would have to describe two shipwrecks in his *history of Portugal*.

> Both these, but especially the first, are so dreadfully distressful, that I look on to the task of dwelling upon all the circumstances, and calling them up before my own sight, and fixing them in my own memory, as I needs must do, with very great reluctance. Fifteen years ago, the more melancholy a tale

was, the better it pleased me, just as we all like
tragedy better than comedy when we are young.
But now I as unwillingly encounter this sort of
mental pain as I would any bodily suffering.

~~~

When Charles Lamb heard the news of John's death,
his reactions – though less self-regarding, more concerned with the Wordsworths' feelings, than those of
Clarkson and Southey were – also involved analysis
of the effect of bereavement and disaster on the
psychology of the bereaved. He and his sister Mary
were struck to the heart by the loss of John, whom
they had admired and felt comfortable with whenever they met. Nobody could be shy or reserved with
the Lambs, and John had felt confidential enough to
show them his 'pleasant exultation ... in the wish
that he might meet a Frenchman in the seas', a
wish that was gratified in 1804 when his convoy of
East Indiamen met and put to flight the French fleet
off the Malay Peninsula. The Lambs would always
remember John as a 'good-humoured happy man'
who had been friendly with them. Yet in Lamb's
mind there was something of that remorse for not
having respected John more in his lifetime, which
William and Dorothy perhaps also felt, and which
caused them to beatify him when they had lost him.
Clear-sighted Lamb knew that this reaction was a
'refinement'. John's death, he said,

always occurs to my mind with something like a feeling of reproach, as if we ought to have been nearer acquainted, and as if there had been some incivility shown him by us, or something short of that respect which we now feel; but this is always a feeling, when people die, and I should not foolishly offer a piece of refinement, instead of sympathy, if I knew any other way of making you feel how little like indifferent his loss has been to us.

His more positive counsel, three days later, was a message of hope. John had been a man of happy temperament, and the Wordsworths must 'cultivate his spirits, as a legacy: and believe that such as he cannot be lost'.

~~~

THE WORDSWORTHS' COUSIN, Captain John Wordsworth senior, a former captain of the *Abergavenny*, wrote to William to condole, in the ceremonious style then considered appropriate, describing the sorrow he and his wife had felt at 'the untimely end of your ever dearly to be remembered and deservedly lamented Brother', but suggesting that 'Time and Resignation to the Divine Dispensation will I trust with the aid of Reflection work a happy Change in your dear Sister's Health and Spirits and gradually restore to you all that Comfort and Happiness which have ever presided in your humble but cheerful Cot.'

After thus putting his young cousins in their place socially, the captain went on more helpfully to quote testimony to John's popularity. 'It will be highly gratifying to know that John was the delight of all the Passengers, had you heard this Praise from the Lips of Mr Evans (a Man of strong sense and discernment) it would have given you as it did me a melancholy Pleasure.' He concluded by saying that however happy John might have been in this life had he survived, happiness was now 'secured to him effectually in the presence of his Creator where there is Joy for evermore'. Lowering the tone with rather a bump, he ended by inviting William to stay, with the assurance that a well-aired bed would await him.

~~~

FOR THE EVANS FAMILY, who had been passengers in the *Abergavenny* at the start of her voyage, and had established a friendly relationship with John, his death was an omen. Thomas Evans, his daughter Emilia and his niece Rebecca survived the wreck, and soon afterwards met Captain John Wordsworth senior in London. Captain Wordsworth had passed on to William and Dorothy the information that Thomas Evans had spoken of John with 'much tenderness', and this encouraged William to write to Evans for an account of his last hours on the ship, and of John's behaviour. Thomas Evans's feeling reply was a great consolation to the Wordsworths; Dorothy transcribed it in full to send to Lady Beaumont. Evans praised John's steadiness, judgement and resolution in the hour of danger, his mild and reflecting character, his kindness to the Evans family which 'endeared him to us when living, and whose memory, when no more, is and ever will be dear to us'.

He added a message from his daughter and niece that they were proud to acknowledge John's attention and care.

A year after her rescue from the *Abergavenny*, Emilia Evans was brave enough to embark once more from England to India, but the waves were again massing on her horizon. There was much bad weather on her voyage, but she reached India safely. Soon after her arrival she married William Scott, a talented young civil servant in the East India Company's service. He was appointed to an up-country station soon after their marriage, and they were travelling there by boat up a river when in the middle of the night the boat began to sink; the water rushed into their cabin, but they managed to escape through the window, minutes before the boat went down. Soon after this Scott became ill, and was told by the doctors that the only hope of his recovery was for him to leave India and go home. He and his wife therefore took passage on the *Calcutta*, a homeward-bound East Indiaman. The *Calcutta* encountered a violent storm in the Indian Ocean, and neither the ship nor those on board were ever heard of again.

Chapter Fourteen

'CHARLES HAS WRITTEN to us the most consolatory letters, the result of diligent and painful inquiry of the survivors of the wreck, for this we must love him as long as we have breath. I think of him and his sister every day of my life, and many times in the day with thankfulness and blessings,' said Dorothy of Charles and Mary Lamb a month after the shipwreck. But there was another, still dearer, friend whose consolations William and Dorothy most of all longed for. Through all their grief about John, they worried about how Coleridge [Plate 16] would suffer when he heard the news. It would distress him to the heart, and he was not strong enough to bear such sorrow, wrote William on the very day on which he himself had heard the news. He was absolutely sure that Coleridge would return to be with them in their grief the moment he heard the news, unless his job in Malta made this impossible. Coleridge knew and loved John, and he also knew, better than anyone else, what John had meant to his family; indeed even the other brothers, Richard and Christopher, did not have the faintest idea of what John had been in himself and to William, Dorothy and Mary; only Coleridge truly understood that. John had been worthy of the friendship of Coleridge; that was among the highest praise that William could accord to his lost brother.

Lamb was well aware how much the Wordsworths would want Coleridge's presence at such a time, and how little in comparison he and his sister could do to make up for Coleridge's absence; he wished he were Coleridge so that he could give the Wordsworths the consolation they needed. Mary Lamb felt this too, and expressed it in an awkward touching poem which she sent to Dorothy.

Why is he wandering o'er the sea?
Coleridge should now with Wordsworth be.
By slow degrees he'd steal away
Their woe, and gently bring a ray
(So happily he'd time relief)
Of comfort from their very grief –
He'd tell them that their brother dead
When years have passed o'er their head,
Will be remember'd with such holy,
True, and perfect melancholy,
That ever this lost brother John
Will be their hearts companion.
His voice they'll always hear, his face they'll always see,
There's naught in life so sweet as such a memory.

Coleridge was not in fact 'wandering o'er the sea' on his way home to England, as all his friends hoped and expected. A year earlier he had sailed to the Mediterranean in hopes of recovering his health, and for the last few months he had been acting as Secretary to the Governor of Malta, Sir Alexander Bell. He meant to return to England in the spring of 1805, as he wrote to the Wordsworths three days before he heard the news of John's death, but the exigencies of his job, and his own fluctuating plans for his future, kept him on the island for many more months.

Coleridge had come to know John Wordsworth well in the last six years. They had gone together on a walking tour with William in the Lakes in 1799, in the course of which Coleridge wrote to Dorothy 'Your Brother John is one of you; a man who hath solitary usings of his own intellect, deep in feeling, with a subtle Tact, a swift instinct of Truth and Beauty. He interests me much.' Coleridge remembered that he, John and William had laughed aloud when they were by Stickle Tarn in Langdale, and had woken an echo from the surrounding hills; William was later to make use of this incident in his poem 'To Joanna', which became John's greatest favourite among his brother's poems.

The following summer Coleridge and John both stayed at Dove Cottage for some months, went bathing together, sailed on the lake reading poems and sat up until midnight chatting with Dorothy after

William had gone to bed. After that Coleridge met John fairly often in London when John was between voyages, and commissioned him to bring back from the East hashish for Tom Wedgwood, and Chinese and Indian drawings for another friend. John showed affectionate solicitude about Coleridge's health; though he continued to be 'very entertaining', he looked poorly, seemed to have lost his former lively spirits, obviously had a 'very bad condition or habit of body' (Coleridge's opium habit had by then become a noticeable addiction, though not to the extent it was later to reach). Coleridge consulted the much-travelled John about the most hopeful parts of the world in which to recover his health; John advised the Azores, where he had once spent two months, as the best place for Coleridge to winter in – it would almost certainly cure his complaints. Coleridge even suggested that he might sail with John on his ship on a China voyage. John was in two minds about this suggestion; it might do Coleridge good, but Italy would be better for him. If Coleridge really wished to go, and if the East India Company would allow a passenger on one of their China-direct ship voyages, which their regulations normally forbade, John would take Coleridge with great pleasure, though he was afraid he would be blamed for taking his friend away from his wife and family for so long.

Clearly John felt it was a risky proposition all round, and it came to nothing, like Coleridge's other projects to winter in the Azores, or in Sicily or Portugal. It was a captivating dream all the same; it would indeed have been an allegorical consonance if Coleridge had sailed to the East in a vessel laden with opium and had set foot on the shore behind which lay Xanadu. Perhaps, though, Coleridge in the end would not have found John quite so instinctively aware of truth and beauty as he had first thought, for John confessed that 'The Ancient Mariner' was a poem he could never bear to read – perhaps it was beautiful, but he could not see the beauty. It was a strange confession for a poetry-loving sea captain to make. There was something ambiguous about his imaginative responses which neither William nor Coleridge could quite categorize; William called him a silent poet, Coleridge saw him as 'John that unperforming observer'.

What actually happened to Coleridge when he heard the news of John's death seems to have been, by his own notebook account written at the time, that he went into the drawing-room of Government House in Valetta, looking for Sir Alexander Ball; he found it full of visitors, and was met by Lady Ball, who asked him if he knew Captain Wordsworth? Coleridge thought she meant the senior Captain John Wordsworth, and replied that he knew him a little. 'Is he not a brother of the Mr Wordsworth you so often talk of?' persisted Lady Ball, and when Coleridge said 'No,' still thinking that she meant the senior captain, Lady Ball went on, 'But have you heard his melancholy fate?' Coleridge turned pale and questioned her further, and she related that the ship, and three hundred of those on board, the captain among them, had gone down. She began to falter when she saw the effect of her news on Coleridge, who could only say 'Yes, it is his Brother' and escape from the room strangling with his emotion, just able to mutter to Sir Alexander that he had heard of the death of a dear friend, and to stagger to his room with the help of the sergeant-at-arms. He spent the next two days at the Governor's summer palace at San Antonio and with a friend in the old Maltese capital Citta Vecchia, entering in his notebook wonderful descriptions of the surrounding landscape and its spring foliage, and then of the street scenes when he returned to Valetta. He was back at work with the Governor five days after hearing the news; it was another two days before he mentioned it again in his notebook.

What he later claimed, and perhaps believed, to have happened was different. He wrote to his wife; 'On being told abruptly by Lady Ball of John Wordsworth's fate I attempted to stagger out of the room (the great Saloon of the Palace with 50 people present) and before I could reach the door fell down on the ground in a convulsive hysteric Fit. I was confined to my room for a fortnight after.' This version, including the fortnight in bed, was circulated by Mrs Coleridge to the Wordsworth circle. Three years later, the event had been still further elaborated in Coleridge's memory; he now described how the news of John's death had reached him in his own room, into which a friend rushed to tell him what had happened, and that this occasioned him to fall heavily backwards onto his head, which so bruised him that ever since then, when he experienced any great agitation, he had 'a feeling of, as it were, a *shuttle* moving from that part of the back of my head horizontally to my forehead, with some pain but more confusion'.

Coleridge was tirelessly interested in the working of his own mental and physical sensations, and what he wrote about John's death was even more concerned with its effect upon himself than with the grief of William and Dorothy. But he did lament their loss with piteous cries: 'O William, O Dorothy, Dorothy! – Mary – and you loved him so!... Dear, dear John!... O God have pity on us! O may Almighty God bless you, my dear Friends! and comfort you.' He mourned the vanishing of John's dream of retiring to live with his brother and sister among the lakes and mountains that he loved. He dwelt on the horrors of shipwreck: 'Dying in all its shapes; shrieks; and confusion; and mad Hope, and Drowning more deliberate than Suicide', which was John's end instead of a peaceful death nursed and surrounded by the women he loved. For himself he despaired of ever seeing home again, he had lost all hope, and only fear was left.

~~~

THE MOST MEMORABLE passages in Coleridge's notebook entries about John's death, and the ones which have caused most discussion and disagreement among the biographers, were his references to Sara Hutchinson in connection with John. Sara had been Coleridge's own beloved for the past six years. Throughout his voyage to Malta and his sojourn there, Sara continued to preoccupy his thoughts, to appear in his dreams at night, to incarnate herself in all that he saw by day. Now she infiltrated his grief over John's death, and he gave her a share in it, in right of a claim which he had never before mentioned, or perhaps even thought of.

A year earlier he had experienced a tormenting vision that Mary Wordsworth might die and that *William* would then marry Sara. The fact that he recorded it in his notebook in cipher suggests that he felt some shame at this unfounded jealousy, and he later admitted that it had been a morbid fantasy. Now his self-torturing self-enhancing imagination made him insert roles for Sara and himself in this new tragedy of John's death, in which he would appear at stage-centre, nobly bearing the crushing loss of Sara. He could experience the glow of offering up a great sacrifice – but would not actually have to make it.

On the day he heard of John's death, he wrote in his notebook, 'O blessed Sara, you who in my imagination at one time I so often connected with him, by an effort of agonizing Virtue, willing it with cold sweat-drops in my brow!' Two months later, another histrionic notebook entry prolonged the role he had assumed. 'O dear John Wordsworth! Ah that I could but have died for you, and you would have gone home, married S. Hutchinson ... O how very, very gladly would I have accepted the conditions. But thou art gone, who mightest have been so happy, and I live.' Like the hysteric fit striking him to the ground when he heard the news of John's death, and the never-healing bruise from his fall, the sacrifice of Sara became part of a picture which was to hang permanently in his hall of delusions, so that three years later he would tell a friend that if John had lived, Sara would have married him.

There is no real evidence, apart from these notebook entries of Coleridge's, that John Wordsworth and Sara Hutchinson were ever betrothed or committed to each other. They had not spent much time in each other's company; Sara was not at Dove Cottage at the same time as John in the 'blessed months' of 1800. They were certainly on friendly terms; John often sent affectionate messages to Sara in his letters to Mary, but they do not sound very different from the messages he also sent to the Hutchinson brothers, unlike the heartfelt warmth with which he wrote to Mary herself, and there are no letters from John directly to Sara. If Sara had any strong feelings about John, they remain, like all her deep feelings about others, hidden away. When the news of John's death reached Grasmere, she hurried to be with her sister and brother-in-law in their sorrow, and did them much good by her presence, as William acknowledged, but this represents her as a comforter of the others rather than as chief mourner, which she surely would have been if she had been engaged to John. A letter of her own, written at this time to the friend, Mrs Cookson, with whom she had been staying when she abruptly left to go to Dove Cottage to help the Wordsworths, is curiously impersonal. All of them, she said, were now well in bodily health, but too heartbroken to enjoy the delightful weather; 'we cannot stir from the house without meeting a thousand fresh reminiscences of our loss' – *our* loss, not *my* loss. Most of her letter is about plans for returning home, and her regrets that she had had to cut short her delightful visit to the Cooksons, which would now be for ever associated with painful recollections. It does not sound like the letter of a woman who has just lost her own dearest love.

It is however very possible that William and Mary Wordsworth would have liked his brother to marry her sister. It would have made still closer the loving community in which they all planned to live when John retired and came to settle in Grasmere. It would have freed Sara from what they were beginning to regard as her bondage to Coleridge, which could have no happy outcome as he was a married man. It would, they may have hoped, supersede John's equally hopeless devotion to Mary. There are some indications that William had this prospect in mind when he included Sara, as one whom John had seen much of, in the circle in which John was to find 'all that was wanting to make him completely happy' when he retired to Grasmere. After John's death William described him as having 'everything in prospect which could make life dear'. If there had been an actual engagement to Sara, William would presumably have been more specific when describing, as he did at such length, every aspect of the hopes that had been lost when the *Abergavenny* went down.

Some of the greatest authorities on the Wordsworths and on Coleridge are convinced that such an engagement existed; others are equally convinced that Coleridge made the whole thing up.

~~~

COLERIDGE SAW a full report on the loss of the ship in the newspaper which Lady Ball sent to him next day, with a note apologizing for the shock she had given him by breaking the news so abruptly; she feared that 'your strong feelings are too great for your health'. This newspaper may have been the *Courier*, which had published an account of the wreck on 7 February, so a copy could have reached Malta by the end of March. A copy of the *Gentleman*'s *Magazine* of February 1805 must also have found its way to Malta, as on 20 April a long account of the wreck, including Cadet Gramshaw's detailed description, published only in the *Gentleman*'s *Magazine*, appeared in the Maltese newspaper *Il Cartaginese*.

Il Cartaginese was an Italian-language journal sponsored by the British authorities in Malta; it was a propaganda weapon intended to counteract the influence in the Mediterranean of the French newspaper *Le Moniteur*; its title was a gesture of defiance towards Napoleon who had boasted that Malta, like Carthage, must be destroyed. Its editor, Vittorio Barzoni, was a friend of Coleridge's, and it has been speculated that Coleridge may have collaborated in the article about the wreck. It is difficult to see his hand in *It Cartaginese*'s turgid and sententious style, but he may have supplied some of the background information. Both the *Courier* and *Il Cartaginese* reported John Wordsworth's words 'God's will be done! let her go' more or less correctly, but in Coleridge's mind they were curiously transformed into 'I have done my duty! let her go'.

When Coleridge finally left Malta for Sicily in September, he saw an old fisherman sitting on a lava rock at Catania who was reading this very issue of *Il Cartaginese* with the account of the *Abergavenny* wreck. Bundles of *Il Cartaginese* were thrown on the shores of Sicily by the British as a propaganda exercise, and it paid the local fishermen to collect them as the French authorities gave a bounty for every copy handed to them. To Coleridge, seeing a mariner on the seashore reading the story of the wreck and its lost men was a symbolic nexus.

The first letter from Coleridge that the Wordsworths received after John's death was hardly full of sympathy for them. It was mainly concerned with his plans for returning to England; the nearest reference he could bring himself to make to their loss was to mention 'events that I dare not at present speak of – but which have wrenched my very heart. O dear Friends! Death has come among us.' In two letters to his wife in July and August he insisted that he did not dare to mention the name of the lost one, it would completely overset him, would make his inmost heart bleed. It was 'as sore a heart-wasting as I believe ever poor creature underwent' he told Southey when he finally got back to England. Such an agony of self-concern invites the question: would he really have been the consoler of the Wordsworths' grief for whom they longed, and in whom Lamb believed? Yet his notebooks in the months between hearing of John's death and his return to England tell a more sympathetic story than his letters. In them he poured out his concern for William, Mary and Dorothy and how they would bear the loss, his admiration of John's courage and devotion to duty. He remembered the family's excitement over John's share in the encounter with the French squadron off Malaya. He had not been with them when they heard the news – he was already in Malta by then – but here too he could not resist writing himself into a central role in the event: 'I was at Grasmere in spirit only, but in spirit I was one of the Rejoicers – as Joyful as any, and perhaps more Joyous!'

It is not these notebook entries of sympathy that show how Coleridge really could have comforted William if they had been together at this time, but the many notebook passages of philosophical and theological speculations arising from John's death, into which Coleridge launched in diary entries during these months. They were on subjects such as the two men had often discussed together, and were what William needed to stiffen and stimulate his mind in a way which none of those around him – neither Dorothy nor Mary, neither Southey nor Beaumont – had the intellectual rigour to supply; only Coleridge's deep thinking could have given him that.

When he first heard the news of John's death, Coleridge was tempted to question whether life had any real meaning or purpose, whether Providence could be beneficent, but he went on to philosophize on destiny and death, on the true nature of love, on religious faith and belief in immortality as one of the 'averred remedies of human sorrows', above all on duty – the duty which he believed John had evoked in his last words – as the real purpose of life in this world, and the 'angelic happiness' of the life to come. He derived his teleology from his observations on how his own mind worked; he admitted that writing about his own feelings was his solace when all else failed. Even this comfort now abandoned him at times, but it is possible to imagine what an alleviation and stimulus his speculations would have been to Wordsworth, who was now beginning to attempt the reconciliation of such an event as the wreck of the *Abergavenny* with conceptions of life's purpose, and to sublimate such a reconciliation in his poetry.

Chapter Fifteen

'HOW DO YOU TURN catastrophe into art?' asked Julian Barnes in *A History of the World in 10½ Chapters*, and went on to analyse the process by which Géricault, meditating on the wreck of a French warship and how its survivors spent fifteen days on a raft before they were rescued, reshaped their experience into the picture which was originally called simply *Scène de naufrage* but which we now always know as *Le Radeau de la Méduse*. Julian Barnes concluded that in the picture 'catastrophe has become art: that is, after all, what it is for'.

~~~

WILLIAM WORDSWORTH'S first attempt to turn the catastrophe of his brother's death into art, to create his own 'scène de naufrage', had been a failure. He had, as has been seen, begun soon after John's death to compose a poem about the disaster, but he had been too much overcome by grief to write down the fragmentary lines he had composed, and too considerate of his sister's and wife's feelings to dictate the lines to them, so the fragments sank from his memory. But when the first agony of sorrow had abated, he found that he could not rest till he had found a way of doing justice to John's renown. At the beginning of April 1805 Dorothy was able to report that William had started writing poetry again. 'Till he has unburthened his heart of its feelings on our loss he cannot go on with other things, and it does him good to speak of John as he was, therefore he is now writing a poem on him.'

It was not directly a poem about John that William yet felt able to write. What he achieved in the last fortnight of April was to add 300 lines to the great work on the growth of his mind that subsequently became known as *The Prelude*. Musing on memories of John, he recalled a moment in their boyhood when he, John and Richard waited on a windy crag by a withered tree for the horses that were to take them home from school for the Christmas holidays. Ten days after they got home, their father died, and William felt this sorrow as a correction by God of the hopes and 'trite reflections of morality' in which he had indulged when he sat on the crag waiting for the horses. John was only indirectly commemorated in these lines recalling an event at which he had been present, but which was mainly intended to reveal how the mind, recalling in memory such 'spots of time', grows and develops as it feeds on them. It was an observation to which William was often to return, as he did now when rain and stormy winds beat on the roof of Dove Cottage at night, and inevitably invoked the tempest that wrecked the *Abergavenny*. Southey had foreseen how the mere sound of the wind would continue to awaken the Wordsworths' recollection of their loss, and for Dorothy it was a recurring source of emotion. At first, surprisingly, it was a feeling of joy that came over her when for the first time she heard the wind howling as she lay in bed, after a spell of placid weather which mocked their grief over John's death; but later she was to own 'what a fearful thing a windy night is now at our house! I am too often haunted with dreadful images of Shipwrecks and the Sea when I am in bed and hear a stormy wind.' William ended the 300 lines he wrote in April with a declaration to Coleridge, to whom the whole long poem was addressed, that the movement of mind – learning to pass on from his trite hopes on the crag to his realization of the world's sorrows when his father died – which John's death had recalled to his memory, had strengthened in him once again the poet's vocation to seek for truth.

In the first two weeks of May, still unable to write a separate poem directly in John's memory, he wrote the concluding books of *The Prelude*, ending with an address to Coleridge recalling their youthful days of wantoning 'in wild Poesy', describing how he had recently been through 'Times of much sorrow, of a private grief/Keen and enduring' which the mind-development that he had described in the poem had enabled him both to feel more deeply and to bear more firmly. Coleridge's imminent return from Malta would be the greatest comfort; when they first met, they would mingle their tears over John's death, and then console themselves by reading William's poem and by confirming their belief in the poet's mission and power to contribute to the redemption of an ignominious age of the world.

This showed how John's death had set William's mind working again, but was not exactly a commemoration of John himself. An incident in early June was to produce that. William set out with a neighbour to fish in Grisedale Tarn; when he got there he remembered that it was here that he and Dorothy had stood to see John hurrying down the mountainside after parting from them at the end of his 1800 visit, when he had to return to London to take command of his ship. William left his companion and composed, in floods of tears, the first of his poems dedicated to John's memory, his *Elegiac Verses in Memory of My Brother, John Wordsworth*. The first verse of this, omitted when the poem was eventually published in 1842, began

> I only look'd for pain and grief
> And trembled as I drew more near.

> But God's unbounded love is here
> And I have found relief.

He found it in the sight of a small purple flower, the moss campion, growing on the place where he had parted from John. It seemed to him to be an 'affecting type' of John, teaching him to suffer grief with calm. The hope that John and he had shared of a blessed day to come when they would all be settled together in Grasmere had

> All vanished in a single word,
> A breath, a sound, and scarcely heard:
> Sea – Ship – drowned – Shipwreck – so it came,
> The meek, the brave, the good was gone;
> He who had been our living John
> Was nothing but a name . . .
> Brother and Friend, if verse of mine
> Have power to make their virtues known,
> Here let a monumental stone
> Stand – sacred as a Shrine;
> And to the few who pass this way,
> Traveller or Shepherd, let it say,
> Long as these mighty rocks endure, –
> Oh do not Thou too fondly brood,
> Although deserving of all good,
> On any earthly hope, however pure!

Writing this poem had already brought some relief to William; Dorothy described him as very cheerful and in better spirits than she would have thought possible at this time. A few days later, he wrote another poem, also set in motion by the sight of a flower, the one that John had seen starring an Isle of Wight field, and described in a letter to Dorothy. 'To the Daisy' was a different style of commemoration of John, a direct narrative of his life and death, with stanzas about the actual wreck and the recovery of John's body. In it William drew no philosophical conclusions about the effect of grief on the growth of the mind, he simply described what happened in language perhaps deliberately naif, like a ballad.

> Ill-fated Vessel! – ghastly shock!
> – At length delivered from the rock,
> The deep she hath regained;
> And through the stormy night they steer,
> Labouring for life, in hope and fear,
> To reach a safer shore – how near,
> Yet not to be attained!

> 'Silence!' the brave Commander cried;
> To that calm word a shriek replied,
> It was the last death-shriek.
> – A few (my soul oft sees that sight)
> Survive upon the tall mast's height;
> But one dear remnant of the night –
> For Him in vain I seek.

> Six weeks beneath the moving sea
> He lay in slumber quietly;
> Unforced by wind or wave
> To quit the Ship for which he died,

(All claims of duty satisfied);
And there they found him at her side;
And bore him to the grave.

Vain service! yet not vainly done
For this, if other end were none,
That He, who had been cast
Upon a way of life unmeet
For such a gentle Soul and sweet,
Should find an undisturbed retreat
Near what he loved, at last –

The neighbourhood of grove and field
To Him a resting-place should yield,
A meek man and a brave!
The birds shall sing and ocean make
A mournful murmur for *his* sake;
And Thou, sweet flower, shalt sleep and wake
Upon his senseless grave.

These two poems were written down for William
by Sara Hutchinson in a notebook originally made by
John and given to the Wordsworths so that they could
transcribe William's poems into it and he could then
take it to sea with him as a constant resource and
refreshment. William now sat with the notebook on
his knee, after Sara had inserted his two poems about
John's death, and turned over the written pages and
the still blank ones, and thought that John would
now never read the notebook, nor could he show the
two poems to Beaumont – they were too melancholy
– or to Dorothy or Mary, they would make tears flow

too fast (but he evidently considered it not too heart-rending for Sara Hutchinson to transcribe them – further evidence that she was not seen as qualified, by being engaged to John, as chief mourner for him). William made another poem to John as he turned over the pages of the notebook: 'Distressful gift!' it began, and it ended with a prayer to God for resignation under His chastening rod which had inflicted the sorrow of John's death.

It was not till the end of the year that William wrote the next poem in which John appeared – or partly appeared. 'Character of the Happy Warrior' was ostensibly written in honour of Nelson, when William heard the news of his death in the Battle of Trafalgar on 21 October. Not all the characteristics attributed to the Happy Warrior were Nelson's; William may have derived some of them from his French friend Michel de Beaupuy, but some, William was later to admit, were inspired by John. He, rather than Nelson, is pictured in the lines about the type of the Happy Warrior as unambitious and dedicated to loving homefelt pleasures; his is the courage in adversity, the purity when surrounded by evil. But perhaps it was William himself who was the Happy Warrior with the power, the highest in human nature, to control and transmute pain and fear, and turn them into good, to make catastrophe into art.

~~~

GOD'S CORRECTION of shallow hopes, God's unbounded love, God's chastening rod – all these poems are pervaded by the philosophical problem of pain and why God inflicts it or allows it. 'It is God's will,' John had said when he heard that his ship could not be saved, and these words were repeated over and over again by everyone commenting on John's last hours. It is rather surprising that they achieved such celebrity, because they were a commonplace of resignation then. Echoing the Lord's Prayer, they rose to the lips of most people in the hour of danger and death. They were used by others in the *Abergavenny* wreck. Cadet Gramshaw, when he was nearly washed into the sea again after hauling himself up to the rigging by a rope, was 'resigning himself to the Will of his Creator' when he was rescued after all. The officer guarding the spirit room from the mutinous seamen was reported as saying, 'If it is God's will that we should perish, let us die like men.' Among the survivors several, like Burgoyne and William White, attributed their escape to Providence, to divine intervention. The Wordsworths' friends, in their letters of condolence about the tragedy, all made the same point. 'So it has pleased Providence,' wrote Clarkson of John's death; Captain Wordsworth spoke of 'resignation to the Divine Dispensation'. Sir George Beaumont, trying to distract William's thoughts by dwelling on the political scene, wrote that 'it is pleasing and awful to observe the great vessel of the universe steadily pushing her course with undeviating serenity – because guided by the perfect hand which governs all and rolls through all things . . . nothing can be perpetrated but by his presumption'. It was a singularly tactless metaphor to have chosen in view of what happened to the progress, anything but undeviatingly serene, of the vessel which took John to his death.

Today the normal reaction to disaster is to think of some human being (other than oneself) to blame and to bring a legal action against; but then there was a general semi-conscious assumption among ordinary people that life had a meaningful pattern controlled by Providence, and that disaster must have been incorporated in the pattern because it served some useful purpose. Some of the men in the *Abergavenny* knew or suspected that her wreck was caused by the hand of the pilot rather than the hand of God. Some of the later comments showed a tremor of bewilderment, as in Barlow's poem about the wreck, as to why 'heaven's immutable yet just decree' should cause storms to spare the pirate but drown the honest merchant like John Wordsworth. But that was not typical of the general feeling that the disaster was, as Laura Sophia Temple put it 'the awful judgment of Thy Hand', the inscrutable but unassailable operation of God's will. It became such a commonplace of response to catastrophe that a Victorian novelist, writing half a century later, could refer to 'the usual complacence about resignation to God's will' as being uttered by a middle-aged spinster condoler.

In 1805 it worked for one spinster nearing middle age. For Dorothy Wordsworth John's words about God's will, when he knew the worst, were endlessly comforting. 'A thousand times have I repeated to myself his last words', she told her brother Christopher in the very first letter she was able to write after hearing the news of the wreck. A month later she could say that it was the will of God that John should be taken away from all care and sorrow, and she continued to dwell on the positive thoughts that John had died when he was at his purest and best, had been spared the sorrows that might have come to him had he lived longer, that his example might teach them to submit calmly to the Divine Will, that he was now enjoying a better and more glorious life in Heaven. Only once did she admit that his death sometimes led her to 'thoughts which are almost like rebellion against the will of Heaven' but she added that she knew and trusted that he had been taken away from this life 'for wise ends'. Her later more active religious life and church observance have been ascribed to her efforts to calm her mind after John's death.

For William it was not so straightforward. He too in some of his letters simply acknowledged that it was the will of God that John should be taken away, but it was a disaster which he could not easily reconcile with any conviction of a divinely-ordered universe. What could the God who could let such things happen really be like?

Examining another representation of catastrophe becoming art, Julian Barnes cited Michelangelo's Sistine Chapel frescoes of the Ark and the anguished figures of those left to perish when the Flood rose to drown all humanity except those in the Ark, and posed the question, 'Should we allow ourselves to postulate Michelangelo the rationalist, moved by pity to subtle condemnation of God's heartlessness?'

God's heartlessness was a lurking idea in William's mind as he wrestled with grief over John's death. He had to fight for the conviction that there was a life to come, in which all such sorrows would be more than compensated, and still more so for the idea that they might have some purpose in earthly life. He wrote to his friends – and no doubt would have spoken to Coleridge had he been within reach – about his doubts. In his first letter to Southey the day after hearing the news, he lamented the miseries of human life; 'surely, this is not to be for ever, even on this perishable planet'. 'Poor blind Creatures that we are!' he wrote bitterly to Richard Sharp when he spoke of the irony of John's efforts to secure the voyage that was to take him to his death. In a key letter to Beaumont he made explicit his misgivings about the role of Providence.

> Why have we a choice and a will, and a notion of justice and injustice, enabling us to be moral agents? Why have we sympathies that make the best of us so afraid of inflicting pain and sorrow, which yet we see dealt about so lavishly by the supreme governor? Why should our notions of right towards each other, and to all sentient beings within our influence differ so widely from what appears to be his notion and rule, if everything were to end here? Would it be blasphemy to say that upon the supposition of the thinking principle being destroyed by death, however inferior we may be to the great Cause and ruler of things, we have *more of love* in our Nature than he has? The thought is monstrous; and yet how to get rid of it except upon the supposition of *another* and a *better world* I do not see.

It was John's death that had led William to these reflections, and the death of such a man was only supportable if one believed in another and a better world to come; 'So good must be better; so high must be destined to be higher'. Otherwise what had once been the brave, the good, the living John would indeed have faded into 'nothing but a name'.

The poems that William wrote about John in 1805 did not show complete conviction of the justification of the ways of God to men. The full reconciliation of this experience of grief was yet to come, but he was gradually seeing more and more how catastrophe can be turned into art, how it is possible to find meaning and purpose in the shipwreck and the dark sky over it.

IN MAY 1806 William went to stay with the Beaumonts in their London house in Grosvenor Square. In the house at the time was Beaumont's painting of *Peele Castle in a Storm [Frontispiece]*, which was due to be exhibited at the Royal Academy summer exhibition that year. 'You will recollect,' wrote Beaumont later to William, 'I did not show you Peele Castle tho it was in the room because I thought it might raise painful sensations in your mind. I did not sufficiently consider how sweet the uses were of your adversity, and what a precious jewel it wore in its head.'

William had noticed what he called Beaumont's delicacy in not leading him to the picture, whose depiction of a ship in difficulties in a storm might give William 'painful sensations' by reminding him of John's death. But William found his way to the picture all the same, either in the Grosvenor Square house or at the Academy private view in May. He did not need or want Beaumont's protective precaution.

He now confronted reality; he learned from it, renouncing the option of escaping from it. He looked long at the picture of calamity, the doomed ship nearing the rugged cliffs, thrust on by hurtling waves and winds under a sky of inky clouds. Its link with John's fate touched him nearly, but gave him a melancholy satisfaction rather than a purely painful sensation; 'the picture was to me a very moving one; it exists in my mind at this moment as if it were before my eyes,' he wrote three months later.

He brooded on the contrast the stormy picture made with Peele Castle as he remembered it when he first saw it in 1794. Then the towering castle ruin on an island off the coast of Lancashire had been bathed in sunshine. Now in Beaumont's picture it was a grim landscape of tempest and imminent shipwreck. The poem that he wrote after leaving the Beaumonts and returning to Grasmere, his *Elegiac Stanzas Suggested by a Picture of Peele Castle, in a Storm, Painted by Sir George Beaumont*, revealed that John's death had brought to conjuncture in the growth of his mind a process which had already been welling up for some years, and which was now directing it into a different channel. This turning point in the growth of his mind which the *Elegiac Stanzas* reveal has been interpreted by some commentators as not simply a new direction in his poetry. It has been seen as a gain in the form of an awakening of his Christian observance and belief in a life to come, or as a loss of vision, an admission that his earliest and finest poetic power was dying away. But most critics would agree that the poem exposes above all that John's death had been a catalyst, which finally confronted him with a different kind of poetic truth. If joy had gone, so had the blindness of eyes closed to the world's sorrows, and in their place had come fortitude to face, and through poetry to convey to the world, the true nature of man's life and how it should be lived.

> I was thy neighbour once, thou rugged Pile!
> Four summer weeks I dwelt in sight of thee:
> I saw thee every day; and all the while
> Thy Form was sleeping on a glassy sea.
>
> So pure the sky, so quiet was the air!
> So like, so very like, was day to day!
> Whene'er I looked, thy Image still was there;
> It trembled, but it never passed away.
>
> How perfect was the calm! it seemed no sleep;
> No mood, which season takes away, or brings:
> I could have fancied that the mighty Deep
> Was even the gentlest of all gentle Things.
>
> Ah! THEN, if mine had been the Painter's hand,
> To express what then I saw; and add the gleam,
> The light that never was, on sea or land,
> The consecration, and the Poet's dream,
>
> I would have planted thee, thou hoary Pile,
> Amid a world how different from this!
> Beside a sea that could not cease to smile;
> On tranquil land, beneath a sky of bliss.

Thou shouldst have seemed a treasure-house divine
Of peaceful years; a chronicle of heaven; –
Of all the sunbeams that did ever shine
The very sweetest had to thee been given.

A Picture had it been of lasting ease,
Elysian quiet, without toil or strife;
No motion but the moving tide, a breeze,
Or merely silent Nature's breathing life.

Such, in the fond illusion of my heart
Such Picture would I at that time have made:
And seen the soul of truth in every part,
A stedfast peace that might not be betrayed.

So once it would have been, – 'tis so no more;
I have submitted to a new control:
A power is gone, which nothing can restore;
A deep distress hath humanized my Soul.

Not for a moment could I now behold
A smiling sea, and be what I have been:
The feeling of my loss will ne'er be old;
This, which I know, I speak with mind serene.

Then, Beaumont, Friend! who would have been
    the Friend,
If he had lived, of Him whom I deplore,
This work of thine I blame not, but commend;
This sea in anger, and that dismal shore.

O 'tis a passionate Work! – yet wise and well,
Well chosen is the spirit that is here;
That Hulk which labours in the deadly swell,
This rueful sky, this pageantry of fear!

And this huge Castle, standing here sublime,
I love to see the look with which it braves,
Cased in the unfeeling armour of old time,
The lightning, the fierce wind, and trampling waves.

Farewell, farewell the heart that lives alone,
Housed in a dream, at distance from the Kind!
Such happiness, wherever it be known,
Is to be pitied, for 'tis surely blind.

But welcome fortitude, and patient cheer,
And frequent sights of what is to be borne!
Such sights, or worse, as are before me here. –
Not without hope we suffer and we mourn.

List of Sources

I. Contemporary letters and diaries

BEAUMONT, Sir George, *Letters to William Wordsworth, 1802–1831*, Wordsworth Library, Grasmere

CLARKSON, Thomas, *Letter to William Wordsworth, 1st March 1805*, Wordsworth Library, Grasmere

COLERIDGE, Samuel Taylor, *Collected Letters*, ed. E. L. Griggs, vol. III, Clarendon Press, 1959

———, *Notebooks*, ed. Kathleen Coburn, vol. II, Routledge & Kegan Paul, 1962

COLERIDGE, Sara, *Sara Coleridge and Henry Reed*, ed. Leslie L. Broughton, Cornell University Press, 1937

GILPIN, Thomas, *Letter to William Wordsworth, 25th April, 1805*, Wordsworth Library, Grasmere

HICKEY, William, *Memoirs*, ed. Alfred Spencer, Hurst & Blackett, 1925

HUTCHINSON, Sara, *Letters, 1800–1835*, ed. Kathleen Coburn, Routledge & Kegan Paul, 1954

KERRIDGE, J. B., *Weymouth and Melcombe Regis and Its Environs*, MS record, Dorset County Library

LAMB, Charles and Mary, *Letters*, ed. E. W. Marre, vol. II, Cornell University Press, 1976

SOUTHEY, Robert, *Life and Correspondence of Robert Southey*, ed. C. C. Southey, vol. II, Longmans, 1850

———, *Selection from the Letters of Robert Southey*, ed. J. W. Warter, vol. I, Longman, 1856

———, *New Letters of Robert Southey*, ed. K. Curry, Columbia University Press, 1965

STEWART, C. H., *Letter to Captain John Wordsworth Senior, 22nd March 1805*, Wordsworth Library, Grasmere

WORDSWORTH, John, *Letters*, ed. Carl H. Ketcham, Cornell University Press, 1969

WORDSWORTH, Captain John Senior, *Letter to William Wordsworth 18th March 1805*, Wordsworth Library, Grasmere

WORDSWORTH William, *Poetical Works*, ed. E. de Selincourt, Clarendon Press, 1947

WORDSWORTH, William and Dorothy, *Letters: The Early Years 1787–1805*, eds E. de Selincourt and C. L. Shaver, vol. I, Clarendon Press, 1967

WORDSWORTH, Dorothy, *Journals*, ed. Helen Darbishire, Oxford University Press, 1958

II. Contemporary newspapers, pamphlets etc., ships' logs, East India Company records

Courier, 5, 7 and 8 February 1805

Morning Chronicle, 2, 8 and 9 February 1805

Morning Herald, 8 February 1805

Observer, 17 February 1805

St James's Chronicle, 7 and 9 February 1805

The Times, 8 February 1805

Gentleman's Magazine, 'Loss of the Abergavenny', LXXV,
    Part I February and March 1805, pp. 174–5, 190, 233,
    294

Il Cartaginese, 'Wreck of the Vessel Called the Earl of
    Abergavenny', Malta Political Journal, 20 April 1805

*An Authentic Narrative of the Loss of the Earl of Aber-
    gavenny, East Indiaman, Off Portland. Corrected from
    the Official Returns at the East India House*, Stockdale,
    London, 13 February 1805

*An Authentic Narrative of the Loss of the Earl of Aber-
    gavenny, East Indiaman, Captain John Wordsworth, Off
    Portland on the Night of Feb. 5 1805. Drawn from
    Official Documents, and Communications from Various
    Sources By a Gentleman in the East India House*,
    Minerva Press, 1805

*A Correct Narrative of the Loss of the Earl of Abergavenny,
    East Indiaman, J. Wordsworth Esq. Commander, Which
    Foundered in Weymouth Roads, on Tuesday Night,
    February 5th 1805*. Cornet G. A. Burgoyne, Harvey,
    Weymouth, n.d.

*A Correct Statement of the Loss of the Earl of Abergavenny,
    East Indiaman, John Wordsworth Commander, Which*

Was Driven Furiously on the Rocks Off the Bill of Portland, February 5 1805, Thomas Tegg, London, n.d.

European Magazine, 'Wyke Regis Church', August 1805, vol. XLVIII, p. 284

BARLOW, John, *The Loss of the Earl of Abergavenny, East Indiaman: A Poem* with Notes, M. Virtue, Weymouth, n.d.

BRAITHWAITE, John, *Journal of the Endeavour, John Braithwaite, Master, An Account of the raising of the cargo of the East Indiaman 'Earl of Abergavenny' lost in Weymouth Bay in 1805*. Weymouth Public Library

TEMPLE, Laura Sophia, *Verses on the Loss of the Abergavenny*, Thomas Tegg, London, n.d.

Court Book, Minutes of the Court of Directors, East India Company, October 1804–April 1805, India Office Library 113A B/140

Captain's Log of Earl of Abergavenny, 1801–2, 1803–4, India Office Library.

Captain's Log of HMS *Weymouth*, January–February 1805, Public Record ADM.51.1547

III. Biographies, critical studies, background

BARNES, Julian, *A History of the World in 10½ Chapters*, Picador, 1990

BERRIDGE, Virginia and Edwards, Griffith, *Opium and the*

People. Opium Use in Nineteenth Century England, Allen Lane, 1981

BYATT, A. S., *Unruly Times: Wordsworth and Coleridge in their Time*, Hogarth Press, 1989

CHAMBERS, E. K., *Samuel Taylor Coleridge: A Biographical Study*, Clarendon Press, 1938

COTTON, Sir Evan, *East Indiaman: the East India Company's Maritime Service*, ed. Charles Fawcett, Batchworth Press, 1949

COURTWRIGHT, David T., *Dark Paradise; Opium Addiction in America Before 1940*, Harvard University Press, 1982

CUMMING, E. M. and Carter, D. J., 'The Earl of Abergavenny (1805), an outward bound East Indiaman', *International Journal of Nautical Archaeology and Underwater Exploration*, 1990, 19. vol. I, pp. 31–3

DAVIES, Hunter, *William Wordsworth: A Biography*, Weidenfeld & Nicolson, 1980

DRAPER, Sarah, *Shipwreck*, Maritime Collection Series, National Maritime Museum, 1992

EHRMAN, John, *The Younger Pitt: The Consuming Struggle*, Constable, 1996

GILL, Stephen, *William Wordsworth: A Life*, Clarendon Press, 1989

GITTINGS, Robert and Manton, Jo, *Dorothy Wordsworth*, Clarendon Press, 1985

GREAVES, Margaret, *Regency Patron: Sir George Beaumont*, Methuen, 1966

GRIGGS, E. L., *Thomas Clarkson: The Friend of Slaves*, Allen & Unwin, 1936

GUNN, Elizabeth, *A Passion for the Particular: Dorothy Wordsworth, A Portrait*, Gollancz, 1981

HERRMANN, Luke and Owen, Felicity, *Sir George Beaumont of Coleorton, Leicestershire*, Leicester Museum and Art Gallery, 1973

HOLMES, Richard, *Coleridge: Darker Reflections*, Harper Collins, 1998

HUGO, Keith, *All Saints Church, Wyke Regis*, Wyke Regis Church Publication Society, 1999

KING-WARRY, Mrs, *Letters about Wyke Regis Church to Gordon Graham Wordsworth and M. McLean, 20th June and 29th July 1932*, Wordsworth Library, Grasmere

LEFEBURE, Molly, *Samuel Taylor Coleridge: A Bondage of Opium*, Gollancz, 1974

LEGOUIS, Emile, *William Wordsworth and Annette Vallon*, Dent, 1922

LUCAS, E. V., *Life of Charles Lamb*, 2 vols, Methuen, 1905

MCADAM, E. L. Jr., 'Wordsworth's Shipwreck', in P.M.L.A. LXXVII, vol. I, 1962

MOORMAN, Mary, *William Wordsworth*, 2 vols, Clarendon Press, 1957 and 1965

MORSE, Hosea B., *Chronicles of the East India Company Trading to China*, 5 vols, Clarendon Press, 1926–9

NAPIER, Priscilla, *Barbarian Eye*, Brasseys, 1995

OWEN, Felicity and Brown, D. B., *Collector of Genius: A*

Life of Sir George Beaumont, Yale University Press, 1988

PARKINSON, C. Northcote, *Trade in the Eastern Seas, 1793–1813*, Cambridge University Press, 1937

PARSSINEN, Terry, *Secret Passions, Secret Remedies: Narcotic Drugs in British Society 1820–1930*, Manchester University Press, 1983

PHILLIPS, C. H., *The East India Company 1784–1834*, Manchester University Press, 1961

PURKIS, John, *A Preface to Wordsworth*, Longman, 1970

DE QUINCEY, Thomas, *Reminiscences of the English Lake Poets*, Dent, 1961

RAND, Frank P., *Wordsworth's Mariner Brother*, Jones Library, Amherst, Mass., 1966

READ, Mark, *Wordsworth: The Chronology of the Middle Years, 1800–1815*, Harvard University Press, 1975

DE SELINCOURT, Ernest, *Dorothy Wordsworth: A Biography*, Clarendon Press, 1933

STOREY, Mark, *Robert Southey: A Life*, Oxford University Press, 1997

SULTANA, Donald, *Samuel Taylor Coleridge in Malta and Italy*, Blackwell, 1969

WHALLEY, George, *Coleridge and Sara Hutchinson and the Asra Poems*, Routledge & Kegan Paul, 1955

WILBERFORCE, Samuel, *Life of William Wilberforce*, John Murray, 1868

WORDSWORTH, Christopher, *Memoirs of William Wordsworth*, 2 vols, Moxon, 1851

WORDSWORTH, Gordon Graham. Unpublished biography of John Wordsworth, Wordsworth Library, Grasmere

Index